Che Cruch

ABOUC

che Leprechaun

No one is sure where Bob Curran comes from. Tradition says that one moment he wasn't there and the next moment he was in County Down. He has, however, held various jobs — including gravedigger, hospital porter, civil servant and teacher — has studied History and Education at the New University of Ulster, and has received a Ph.D. in Educational Social Psychology. Bob has a strong interest in local history and folklore, and has both written and lectured on these subjects; he is a frequent contributor to radio, and has appeared on television co-presenting programmes on heritage and history. It is said that Bob currently lives somewhere in North Antrim, with his teacher wife and two small children; but it is difficult to be sure, as he is seen only 'between the lights' (at twilight), and then only by a fortunate few.

For Mary, my extremely patient wife,
and for Michael and Jennifer, my own two leprechauns

The Truth

About

the Leprechaun

Bob Curran

WOLFHOUND PRESS

First published 2000
Reprinted 2002

Wolfhound Press
An imprint of Merlin Publishing
16 Upper Pembroke Street,
Dublin 2
Ireland
publishing@merlin.ie
www.merlin-publishing.com

British Library Cataloguing-in-Publications Data.
A catalogue record for this book is available from the British Library.

ISBN 0-86327-800-0

10 9 8 7 6 5 4 3 2

Cover Illustration and Design: Jon Berkeley
Typesetting: Wolfhound Press
Printed by Cox & Wyman Ltd., Reading, Berks, England

Contents

Introduction

THE LEPRECHAUN
IN THE WIDER FAIRY WORLD

Up the airy mountain,
Down the rushy glen,
We daren't go a-hunting,
For fear of little men.

(William Allingham)

Almost every culture has its supernatural beings — from the German ḳobolds (a bad-tempered, diminutive race who live far underground and are extremely hostile to mankind) to the Cherokee nunnehi (tiny, mischievous creatures who live in ancient mounds; they play tricks, but they also look after lost children and guide them home) and the English fairies (tiny sprites who dwell in trees and rivers and who maintain an ambivalent attitude to the human race). Yet perhaps no other people have differentiated between the various forms of supernatural entities as clearly as the Irish. Our folklore and traditions portray a whole range of mysterious and sometimes exotic beings that have interacted with humankind across the centuries.

Strictly speaking, the fairy-creatures of Irish folklore belong to the Otherworld — an ill-defined realm that exists just beyond mortal sight. They coexist with humankind throughout the rural countryside, but generally remain invisible to human eyes. Collectively, they are referred to as the Sídhe (meaning 'dwellers of the mounds' — the word *sí* or *sidh* originally meant 'a mound') or Tuatha de Danann (the followers of the goddess Danu — from an ancient legend in the twelfth-century Book of Invasions); but, across the years, they became known in country folk-tales simply as 'the little people'. This implied a diminutive size and brought the Sídhe into line with other legends to be found in many other cultures across the world.

'At one time they were as tall as you or I,' an old man in County Fermanagh once told me. 'But that was when they were at the height of their power and were greatly feared all across the world. They were gods then, do you see? When the people stopped believing in them and stopped worshipping them, they began to shrink away until they reached their present size. That's why they are so small nowadays.'

There is much to be said for this theory. The venerable Book of Armagh states categorically that these beings were 'the spirits of earth and air' and that they were worshipped right across Ireland. As Christianity spread across the country, the fear and mystery of the fairy folk gradually diminished; and with it, so did the stature of the former gods.

Other traditions, especially in the north of Ireland, hold that the fairies were fallen angels. The legend says that during the great revolt in Heaven, when Lucifer rebelled against the sovereignty of God, some angels 'sat on the fence' and refused to become involved. When Lucifer and his acolytes were defeated and cast into the burning pit, the fate of these indifferent angels was uncertain; they were not good enough to be allowed back into Heaven and not evil enough to be cast into Hell. St Michael reputedly interceded for them, and they were placed on earth, midway between Paradise and the Infernal Regions. Gradually, deprived of their heavenly status, they began to dwindle in stature and thus formed the fairy throng.

'They were angels, sure enough,' said an old woman in North Antrim, 'but they would not stand with God against the Devil, and so they were put into the world of men. They became the fairies over a time.'

The fairies were believed to be a very diverse species. Some lived in the air, some on the land, others in the sea, and others still under the earth — and each kind acquired some of the characteristics of their environment. The fairies of the air, for instance, were light, graceful and rather nebulous beings, often described as flitting about on gossamer-like wings. Those who lived in the sea were sometimes covered in fur, like the seals which they clearly resembled, or in scales, like fish. Those who lived on or under the earth were different again. The invisible beings who lived in the raths and earthen forts which littered the countryside were tall and splendid beings — very like humans, it was said, but with an unearthly beauty about them. The fairies that lived under the earth — in mounds and caverns, in ditches and under hedgerows — were small, stunted beings with hard skins and even harder looks. They were often described as being 'as brown as the earth' from their rather harsh environment.

As well as taking on the physical characteristics of their environment, many fairies also acquired a temperamental quality which reflected their surroundings. Fairies of the air were shallow, fickle creatures who changed their minds as often as the wind changed; the moods of water-fairies fluctuated with the tides; and those who dwelt under the earth and in remote places were usually surly and reclusive in their ways. Many were extremely hostile towards humans and went out of their way to do mischief and inflict harm upon unwary mortals.

Much later, probably in the late eighteenth and early nineteenth centuries, a more sophisticated folklore began to divide the fairy realm into two distinct camps. One camp consisted of the trooping fairies — what the poet W.B. Yeats has called the Macara Shee, the fairy cavalcade: a band of supernatural beings, usually of diminutive size, who travelled the country roads on certain nights of the year, such as Hallowe'en and May Eve. At such times, according to rural folklore, the doors of the fairy hills and mounds swung open and the troop came out, led by a king and queen. Depending upon whom they met upon the road, they responded with largesse or with disdain, sometimes rewarding kindness, at other times punishing evil deeds. However, warned the wise people of the countryside, it was as well to avoid them whenever possible and to keep off the moonlit roads as soon as the sun went down.

The other half of fairydom was what Yeats and others referred to as 'the solitary fairies': those supernatural beings who lived well away from humans and from other fairies and had very little to do with them. These beings dwelt in caves, holes, bogs and ditches and remained invisible for most of the time. Mortals could sense their presence only when the fairy lured them into some danger (possibly resulting in death) or when the fairy was accidentally heard by some passer-by. Amongst these solitary creatures were such entities as the banshee (a 'woman of the fairies' who cried for those who were about to die), the linahan shee (the fairy lover who lured men to their doom), the dullahan (a terrible headless figure who galloped through the night bringing doom, misery and destruction to the houses that he passed) and the leprechaun (the fairy shoemaker).

While the banshee has passed, more or less, into ghost-lore, and beings such as the dullahan and the linahan shee have been all but forgotten, the leprechaun has acquired a status which has put him at the forefront of Irish fairy-tales and folk-tales.

Despite his solitary nature, the leprechaun appears to have been seen frequently in many parts of Ireland. Indeed, so generic is the term that almost any other-worldly or supernatural creature is accorded the name 'leprechaun'. Furthermore, the leprechaun has become something of a symbol of Ireland itself (one might be tempted to say he is the 'national elf'). He appears on tea-towels, on linen, in porcelain ornaments and illustrated plates from the Emerald Isle. He has appeared in both films and cartoons as the only fairy sprite in Ireland.

This does both the leprechaun and the fairy world a disservice, for the creature also appears in neighbouring parts of the world — in Scotland, in the Western Isles and in the North of England — and he forms part of a wide panoply of magical beings.

Most of the painted representations of the leprechaun show him to be a jolly, amiable and carefree creature. He is the sort of sprite with whom one would like to share a winter's night beside a roaring fire, listening to his old, humorous tales and sharing his poteen. He is the epitome of Irish hospitality and Irish storytelling.

The leprechaun is anything but amiable and humorous. He is dark and sombre, with little or no levity about him. Nor is he particularly good company, for he seems to carry the woes of the world with him. Leprechauns are also great misers and extremely selfish, so there is little chance of them sharing anything, let alone their stores of poteen. Not only this, but leprechauns on the whole are extremely spiteful; they are as likely to perform an evil trick on the unwary mortal as a helpful or kindly one.

The exception to this rule occurs in some parts of Munster, where, once in a while, a more amiable leprechaun will sometimes present an individual with a *sparán na scillinge* (purse of the shilling) — a marvellous pouch which never becomes empty. However, although it is a wonderful present, there is a malicious reason for this particular gift. Those to whom it is given invariably misuse it — usually becoming drunkards and gamblers — and eventually all their wealth turns to dust and ashes. The leprechaun's present turns out to be a double-edged sword.

Because of their uncivil nature and innate hostility towards humans, leprechauns frequently had to be placated by the householders of the area. Failure to do so would invite mischief upon both family and property. Offerings of milk, cheese, bread and other foodstuffs, as well as twists of tobacco, were sometimes left outside cottage doors at night, to keep the leprechaun from making mischief against the owner or tenant of the dwelling. Fresh water, the dregs of the teapot or a glass of strong liquor were often left out as well. Sometimes libations of whiskey were left on the doorstep, but this alcoholic gift could have an adverse effect upon the sprite.

'Never leave too much whiskey for the leprechaun,' conventional rural wisdom states, 'for if you do, he'll only get very drunk and create a commotion around your house.' It is also said that the whiskey may addle his wits and make him even more malignant than he already is. Leprechauns have to be treated carefully, even when one is offering them presents!

Ancient tradition said that the Tuatha de Danann were usually invisible beings who existed, unseen by mortals, amongst the raths and forts of the countryside. The same is true of the leprechaun, who went about his business beyond the human gaze. The only sign of his presence was, perhaps, a small whirlwind or cloud of dust. In former times (and, in some areas, up until the present day), old men would doff their hats and old ladies would drop a small curtsy as one of these small dust-storms swept past. In some areas, it was also common to genuflect and say 'God bless me', or to throw your left shoe after the cloud; if you did, the leprechaun would be compelled to drop whatever he was carrying — which, if fortune was smiling, might be a bag of gold!

These pillars of dust might also be a sign that the leprechauns were carrying some unfortunate human off to the fairy realm. Leprechauns seem to have had a fondness for abducting unbaptised human babies, which they then sold into service in the various raths and mounds. To protect children from such wiles, it was necessary to have an infant baptised by a clergyman as quickly as possible. In some more remote areas where clerics were not readily available, the midwife who delivered the infant could perform an interim baptism using the following formula:

No seed of fairy, no seed of the hosts of the air, no seed of the world's people can lift away this tranquil little sleeper for whom is made this beneficent prayer of baptism. Evil cannot lie on him [sign of the Cross]; *envy cannot lie on him* [sign of the Cross]; *malice cannot lie on him* [sign of the Cross]. *The two arms of mild Mary, the Mother of God, graciously encompass him; the two arms of the gentle Christ shield, surround and succour this joyous little sleeper of the baptism.*

This particular baptism was used by midwives and 'knee-women' as far away as the Western Hebrides to protect newborn infants from the taran — a specific type of leprechaun-like creature — and a version of it is mentioned in Alexander Carmichael's *Carmina Gadelica*.

Two similar non-clerical protective baptisms reputedly come from the west of Ireland, although they are also found in various parts of Scotland:

When the image of the God of Life is brought into the world, I put three little drops of water on the child's forehead. I put the first little drop in the name of the Father (and the watching women say 'Amen'); I put the second little drop in the name of the Son (and the watching women say 'Amen'); I put the third little drop in the name of the Spirit (and the watching women say 'Amen'). And I beseech the Holy Three to lave and to bathe the child and to preserve it to Themselves, protecting it from any evil thing — witch, goblin or evil spirit. Let no dark thing come near to it or disturb its rest (and the watching women say 'Amen').

The second baptism employs roughly similar language and imagery:

The little drop of the Father
On thy little forehead, beloved one.

The little drop of the Son
On thy little forehead, beloved one.

The little drop of the Spirit
On thy little forehead, beloved one.

To aid thee from the fays,
To guard thee from the host.

To aid thee from the gnome,
To shield thee from the spectre.

To keep thee for the Three,
To shield thee, to surround thee.

To save thee for the Three,
To fill thee with the graces.

The little drop of the Three,
To lave thee with the graces.

If any of the above baptisms was performed by the midwife, then the crafty leprechauns (or any other fairy or witch, for that matter) had no power over the child. Of course, a full clerical baptism had to be performed as soon as possible, but the above incantations had the power to restrain all members of the fairy kind until this could be achieved.

If neither cleric nor midwife was present at the birth, all the father of the child had to do was throw his coat or an item of his clothing over the sleeping infant. This, presumably, was to remind the fairy world that the child had been claimed by the human world, until a cleric could arrive.

Even then, it was believed that children still might not be safe from the leprechauns. Small children were strongly advised not to address a leprechaun directly, or to give direct answers to any questions which the creature might ask, since doing so would place the mortal in the fairy's power; he or she could be whisked off in a magic wind, to be sold in a fairy market or at the door of some rath or mound.

Far from being the jolly little fellow who appears on postcards and ornaments from Ireland, then, the leprechaun is a surly, miserly, mischievous and antisocial being. Rather than being sought out by mortals, he was more likely to be feared.

Nevertheless, he played a central role in the fairy world, and he deserves to be studied in a bit more depth. It is to this study that we now turn.

Chapter One

Origins and General Appearance

Although the fairy kind in general are believed to be descended either from the Tuatha de Danann or from fallen angels, some of their number may have more specific origins. The leprechaun may be one of these distinct entities. So where did leprechauns come from?

Despite its now-widespread appeal — it is used to refer to almost any Irish fairy — the term 'leprechaun' was not really used until the late seventeenth or early eighteenth century. Even then, the word had many different, localised variations. In east Leinster, for example, the term was *liomreachán*, while in south Leinster it was *lúracán*; in Ulster it was *luchramán*, in Connacht *lúracán*. Even within provinces, the name varied. For instance, in parts of Munster, the sprite was called a *luchargán*, *lurgadán* or *cluricán*, while in other areas the description *luchorpán* prevailed.

Many of these descriptions were taken from the sprite's alleged powers or characteristics. Within these terms, there are echoes of the ancient Irish words *luch* (mouse), *lúth* (agility), and *lurga* (ankle). The leprechaun was, therefore, believed to be about the size of a mouse, with speedy reflexes and large feet. The term 'leprechaun' is thought to have been used only in the north Leinster area until the middle or end of the last century. Nowadays, this form seems to be widely used all over Ireland.

The origin of the term 'leprechaun' is complex. It has been argued that it derives from *leith bhrógán* (half-shoe-maker — maker of half a pair of shoes), making the sprite a cobbler by profession, with a corpus of related folklore attached to him. However, it is more likely that the name comes from the ancient Irish *luchorpán* (little man) or *luacharmán* (pygmy), simply denoting a creature of very small stature. In texts dating from the eighth century, the term is used to denote members of a diminutive race. In the legend of Fearghus mac Léide, for example, reference is made to a community of diminutive people who possess magical powers and skills. Fearghus seizes three of them, and, in return for their release, they bestow the magical skills of swimming upon him. Later texts, dating from the tenth, eleventh and twelfth centuries, say that these beings may also bestow certain magical objects, such as silver shoes, which enable a person to walk on water without drowning.

Is the leprechaun, then, a member of such a community? If so, what were the origins of these tiny folk?

Origins — Grogochs, Pechts and Other Creatures

The Irish leprechaun may be part of a much wider lore concerning diminutive races. This lore includes brownies, gnomes, goblins, *fées* and pixies, all of whom feature prominently in Celtic vernacular mythology. It is quite possible that many of the tales concerning leprechauns were adapted by the Irish from other sources, perhaps from outside their own shores. Since there is no reference to the *luchorpán* in Ireland before the seventh or eighth century, there seems little doubt that he was imported from elsewhere and was integrated into native mythologies. But where could these tales have come from?

There is no way to determine an actual source, but it may be that they came from Europe with waves of invaders who gradually settled in Ireland. Right across the Continent, we find tales of small, elusive aboriginal races dwelling in communities well away from their taller counterparts. Some of these little people were considered to have special powers; many are said to have lived underground, and many were believed to be ugly or slightly deformed (or different from humankind) in some way. Might these have been the prehistoric prototypes for the leprechaun?

A clue to the origins of the *luchorpán* comes from Ulster. Here, the leprechaun is known by two quite specific names — 'grogoch' and 'pecht'. It is the latter epithet, 'pecht', which hints at the origin, for it is too close to the word 'pict' — a generic name in the area for aboriginal Scottish peoples — to be simply coincidence. Old local people, particularly in the North Antrim area, are quite sure of the area from which their diminutive neighbours came to Ireland.

'The pechts and grogochs came from Scotland, surely,' stated Robert McCormick, an old man from the town of Ballycastle on the northern coast. 'They came here by way of a land-bridge which was between Kintyre and Antrim in the old days. When the Celtic people came to Scotland, they drove the pechts in front of them and they had to get out of the country. So they came to Ireland, where nobody was living at the time, and started to live here. The Celtic people followed them across the bridge and started to live here too. So the pechts had to hide away in secret places around the countryside, and that's why you never see much of them. That bridge of land is long gone, but the pechts are still here. We call them "fairies" and "wee people", and that's how they came to North Antrim and to Ireland as well.'

Setting aside some of the more fanciful details, there may be some truth in this notion. Both Scottish and Hebridean folklore are filled with tales of communities of little folk living in remote places, some of whom may have migrated to Ireland in prehistoric times. Some of these may well have been aboriginal peoples who were displaced by incoming Celtic settlers. Indeed, the general descriptions of the grogochs or pechts seem to confirm this notion.

Although they are widely regarded as a type of leprechaun, the grogochs differ from the standard leprechaun in appearance and character. They are small and brutish-looking, with flat faces and large, languid eyes. They do not wear clothes; instead they grow long, reddish, matted fur which covers their entire bodies. They are untidy and dirty in their habits — their fur, for example, is tangled with twigs and straw which the grogochs inadvertently pick up on their travels.

'When I was a wee child and staying with my granny in the Glens [of Antrim],' recalled the famous Waterfoot historian and storyteller, Mary Stone, 'we would come in from the fields and my granny would say, "Ye look like an oul' grogoch." I never knew what that meant, but she always started to comb and untangle my hair. Later on, I found out that it meant "untidy", because the grogoch is always very untidy and dirty in his habits. He always has bits and pieces of straw and chaff in his hair, and I suppose that after a day playing in the hay-fields, I was dirty and untidy too.'

Their dwellings were usually piles of tumbled rocks, sometimes no more than two great standing stones pushed over to provide a rude shelter from the elements. Several of these 'grogoch's houses' still exist on Rathlin Island, off the Northern Irish coast.

'The Groigock's [sic] House is two big stones near Leg-an-thass-nee,' reported Rathlin man Frank Craig. 'They said you would have been fit one time to see [once could see] the groigocks lying out on the grass and sunning themselves there. It's up near the Knockans. There used to be plenty of them up there. Leg-a-goin, too: they'd be out sunning themselves, clear as day. When it rained, they took shelter in the House. Two stones leaning together. It's there yet.'

Unlike the majority of the leprechaun species, the grogoch does not possess an overly surly nature. This makes him different even from those leprechaun-fairies whom he most closely resembles — the laughremen of the South Armagh region (small, hairy creatures who possess eminently unsociable dispositions and some-times play tricks upon or show violence towards humankind) and an unspecified fur-covered entity who dwells in remote areas of County Sligo (who continually torments both animals and small children). In fact, the grogoch is usually helpful to the point of being a nuisance, and will sometimes attach himself to one particular individual or household for whom he has developed a special affection. In former times, grogochs would help both Rathlin and North Antrim farmers with the harvest. They were tireless workers; however, they could not tolerate laziness or idleness in others and frequently took steps to rouse a dozing farmhand or careless worker. Frank Craig relates a story from Rathlin which demonstrates this particular fairy trait:

There was a groigock in John Vawnilds' place over in the Castle Quarter [also known as Bruce's Castle]. *He was a wee hairy man who would do turns about the place for John and his wife; he would wash spuds for them and take home the cows of an evening.*

Now, at this time, John was an old man and liked his rest well enough, especially on a Sunday morning when he should have been at mass. He would take a bit of a lie-in after a week's hard work. But the groigock wouldn't have that at all. When old John was lying snoring in the bed, he would hoist himself up onto the covers and creep up. Then he would batter the old man about the face until he got up and did a bit of work before going to mass. They can't stand anyone not working, do you see?

It was the same when the boys in the fields would sit down to have a rest or a can of tea as they did in the olden days. The groigocks would creep up behind them and torment them until they had to go back to the threshing or whatever they were doing. It got so that the groigocks were great pests and the farmers wouldn't want them about, no matter how good workers they were. And poor John Vawnilds had reason to curse them as well.

That's a true story, for I mind [remember] *my grandfather telling that story often. Of course, you don't see groigocks about any more, so I suppose them that sleep late in their beds or in the hay-fields are safe enough.*

Unlike the standard leprechaun, the grogoch was widely thought to be extremely stupid — a kind of North Ulster 'village idiot'. Always eager to please, grogochs would sometimes make a mess of the tasks which they were given, if only through their enthusiasm. A story which was widely told in the Ballycastle area made this point:

A shepherd who worked on Knocklayd Mountain had to come into Ballycastle on business. It was the first time in over a year that he had been away from his herd, and, as he was going to be all day in the town, he had to find somebody to look after his flock. The sides of the mountain are very steep, and young lambs would be wandering all over the place and falling into ravines or sinking into bogs. Somebody had to be there to see that they came to no harm and to round them up if need be.

On the top of Knocklayd, there was an old grogoch living, and he was very friendly and helpful, so the shepherd went up and asked him if he would look after the sheep and lambs. The grogoch came to the mouth of his cave and told him that he'd be delighted to do so. The shepherd took him down the mountainside and showed him the sheep, grazing on the slopes, and the pen into which they would have to be put at night. The grogoch told him not to worry and that everything was safe in his hands.

The next morning, the shepherd took himself off to Ballycastle, leaving the grogoch in charge. Before he left, he told the fairy that he should gather all the sheep and lambs in that night, and he wasn't to let any wander down onto the lower slopes. Again, the grogoch told him not to worry — he had been herding sheep off and on for hundreds of years — and so the shepherd eventually set off for the town.

He was far longer in Ballycastle than he'd planned to be. The business took up most of the day, and then he ran into some old friends who took him to the pub and bought him drink. The crack among them was good, and so it was late when the shepherd set out and nearly morning when he arrived back on Knocklayd Mountain.

To his surprise, all the sheep and their lambs

were in the pen, with the grogoch looking after them. However, the little man seemed greatly out of breath and looked very tired. The shepherd naturally asked him if he'd had any trouble with the flock.

'No real trouble,' the grogoch answered him. 'I got them all gathered in without too much trouble, although a wee brown lamb wouldn't go into the pen and I had to chase it all over the mountain nearly all night. I caught it at last and put it in the pen with the others, but it took me some time to get it in, all right. It didn't want to go.'

This puzzled the shepherd, for he knew that there was no brown lamb among his flock, and he told the grogoch so. The other, however, insisted that the brown lamb was there and brought the shepherd over to the pen to see it. Imagine his astonishment when he saw, lying in the shadow of the circling stone wall, nothing more than a small, out-of-breath hare! The stupid grogoch, unable to tell the difference between a lamb and a hare, had chased it all over Knocklayd for the whole night!

(Traditional North Antrim tale
from the author's own sources)

In spite of their stupidity, the grogochs were extremely good-hearted and eager to do good turns. Indeed, they were so eager to please that they invariably became pests about the house. They would run about (often invisibly) trying to do small chores for the woman of the house, and would usually end up creating more mess than they cleared. When a housewife unaccountably stumbled or tripped in the kitchen, she was sure that she had stepped on or bumped against an invisible grogoch. The great Rathlin Island storyteller Rose McCurdy mentioned such an encounter:

Did nobody tell you about the gruogock? That's what they call them on this island, and on parts of the mainland as well. I had a man from the County Sligo come to see me, and he knew what it was. In Ireland, where I come from [the inhabitants of Rathlin Island always refer to the mainland as 'Ireland'; Rose was born in Glenshesk, outside Ballycastle], *they called him the grigock, but it's this land* [Rathlin] *that I'm talking about now.*

There was a grigock's house up at Clegganleck on the upper end of the island. He was supposed to come down from it every day at one time − Alex Morrison or Owney Murphy will tell you the truth of it, for they seen him many a time. The woman of the house was polluted with the grigock coming down to her every day. When she got up from her chair, he would rise up with her and would be round her legs and feet. And he was always running round the fire and getting in her way. She was polluted.

One day, she was carrying a kettle of boiling water from the fire and the grigock was running around her feet, and what did she do but spill a drop on him. He let out a screech of a yell, they said, and shouted in the old Irish (which was all that he spoke), 'Oh! Oh! My viggerald-vaggerald is all scalded!' That's what it sounded like. And he ran out of the house and all the way back to Clegganleck. But I'll go bail that the grigock never came back to that house again, nor did he go near any of the houses after that.

Unlike other leprechauns, the grogoch was not interested in either money or reward for his labours. In fact, any sort of money or gift was anathema to him, and to offer him such a reward, even out of gratitude or sympathy, would invariably drive him away from a house. Frank

Craig elaborated on this in a famous tale of the grogoch, widely repeated on Rathlin Island.

There was a grogoch worked over at Douglas Cecil's place at times during the year. One time, there was a very harsh winter, with snow lying all over the island, but the grogoch came down from his house and worked away. Old Mrs Cecil — her that's long dead — that was the woman of the house, took pity on him and said that it was a shame to have the grogoch doing everything for them and not getting a haet [anything] back for his troubles, and him such a good worker and all, and the weather being so cold. So she was spinning this day and had a wee bit of the wool left over from what she was making. She thought that she'd make something for the grogoch. There was enough wool to make a pair of heavy socks for him, and she left them out the next time he came by.

When he got them he began to cry.

'Do you not like them?' asked old Mrs Cecil.

And the answer that he gave her was that he could never get back again. 'When yous give me a reward,' says he, 'I can never come back again. I can't get back.'

And he went away crying. That was the last that the Cecils or anyone else saw of him ever again.

The nature and stories of the grogoch have been explored here in some depth, as the creature may give some hint as to the origins of the leprechaun. The primitive conditions in which the grogoch lives — under standing stones, in caves or in deep ravines — are suggestive of a reclusive, aboriginal race who may have migrated to Ireland from Scotland or elsewhere, and who coexisted with the Celtic peoples for a long time. Their overall appearance adds to this theory. There are a number of stories of grogochs working for and trading with country people, and this may be some sort of memory of the interchange between the two races in some former time. Moreover, the grogoch belongs to a tradition of small people and diminutive communities which is widespread all over Scotland and the Hebrides.

Not all such races are deemed to be as slow-witted or as good-hearted as the grogoch − indeed, some are considered to be very wise and crafty in their ways. On the Hebridean island of Colonsay, legends of a particular brownie abound. Although no description of him exists, he is believed to be a small old man who lives in a secluded part of the island, or on one of the neighbouring tidal islands, Oronsay or Cara. It was thought that island witches sometimes consulted this fairy in order to find out future events or to locate lost property within the community. Other tales make him the moral over-seer of island life: those who have wronged their neighbours are sure to be punished by the brownie; those who are neglectful of their work may receive a sharp reprimand (in the form, perhaps, of a small accident or mishap) to remind them of their duties. In order to keep on the right side of the sprite, local people would leave an offering for him − a libation of milk or whiskey − at a large rock near the centre of Colonsay. The method of making this offering was quite specific. The person offering the libation came to the place at night, poured it into a hollow in the middle of the rock and then walked away. On no account should he or she look back, for fear of seeing the brownie and inviting bad luck upon himself or herself − for the little man had miraculous powers and could call down a curse upon the viewer. Invariably, the offering disappeared.

Similar beings, all with peculiar magical skills, existed on many other islands in the Hebrides. The celebrated

Hebridean pirate, Rúairí MacNeill of Barra, is believed to have consulted a little fairy man on the island of North Uist before several of his raids. At the end of the sixteenth century, MacNeill had received Letters of Marque and Reprisal from the English court to enable him to attack French and Dutch shipping. After consulting with the fairy-creature, however, he changed his tactics: he began to attack Irish shipping and ravaged townships all along the coast of Cork. This brought him to the attention of Queen Elizabeth I, who complained of the pirate's activities to King James VI of Scotland. The Scottish king designated Roderick MacKenzie, who afterward became the Tutor of Kintail, to hunt MacNeill down. The little man in North Uist, however, assured the pirate that he would never be captured, and MacNeill had the misfortune to believe the word of a fairy. He was captured by MacKenzie at Kismul Castle on Barra; and, though his life was spared and he was allowed to keep his lands, he had to acknowledge MacKenzie as his overlord and give up piracy, which had been a profitable source of income for him. Legend says that the island of North Uist rang with the spiteful laughter of the fairy man: he had humbled the MacNeill noble, which had been his intention all along.

Throughout the Outer Hebrides, such creatures are known either as *talla* (a Highland Gaelic word for echoes, since they are supposed to be reflections or echoes of humankind) or *iridich nan creag* (the gnomes of the rock). They live in small communities or as solitary fairies, keeping well away from human places, for which they have a particular aversion. They are regarded as being extremely spiteful, seeking only to cause mischief amongst humankind. In appearance, they often resemble the traditional stereotype of the Irish leprechaun, and it may well be that the image of the Irish fairy is derived from his Scottish counterpart. Certainly, he belongs to a general corpus of folklore which stretches between the two countries.

The leprechaun has also connections on the Isle of Man, where a fairy known as the Little Old Man of the Barn exists. This sprite is extremely reclusive, but, like the grogoch in North Antrim, he is extremely helpful to farmers around the Peel area of the island. He works only at night, threshing corn in farmers' barns in return for a libation of milk or whiskey or for a small portion of food. He is also to be greatly feared, for, when crossed or angered, he can cause drought or sickness in live-stock. Generally, however, he is a beneficent spirit and will only react maliciously if someone refuses to leave his offering or acts irresponsibly within the community.

The leprechaun may have another point of origin, this one within the Viking world.

The Norsemen had a highly developed mythology which included giants, monsters, wizards, fighting men and diminutive races. Their dwarfish races — simply known as dwarves — were extremely wise and skilled and worked mainly as ironsmiths. They constructed magical helmets, armour and chains, which adorned many of the Scandinavian heroes. They dwelt far under the earth in volcanic pits (which were their forges) and kept well away from surface-dwellers. However, they could be consulted by and offer advice to other races when the need arose. For example, when the wolf-demon Fenris tormented Asgard (the seat of the Norse gods), the deities asked the dwarves to forge an un-breakable chain which would bind the creature for eternity. This the dwarfish smiths did, using exotic substances such as the spittle of birds and the beard of a woman; and, using the magical chain, the gods were eventually able to bind Fenris.

Dwarves also appear in some of the other Viking sagas, and they are regarded as extremely wise, if somewhat devious, creatures. They were also believed to be the final custodians of arcane knowledge and practices.

Such beings eventually became incorporated into the folklore of other races. For example, the Viking dwarves probably metamorphosed into the trows of Orkney and Shetland — small, usually solitary, highly malignant creatures who inhabited remote islands and sites scattered all through the Northern waters. Trows are believed to be extremely ugly and dirty; they may help humans if they have a mind to, but they are more likely to create some mischief. They are also often regarded as being extremely drunken in their ways, and this may reflect their Viking origins — Viking dwarves were always paid with a jug of mead or spirit.

So how did Viking folklore come to influence the folk beliefs of Ireland?

Between the ninth and eleventh centuries, Ireland was probably one of the most important Norse bases in the Sudreyjar (the Southern Sea). A number of large Viking colonies existed, mainly in the south of the country; these were the forerunners of such modern cities as Dublin, Limerick, Waterford, Wexford and Cork. From these colonies, raiding ships sailed out to wreak havoc against shipping and settlements along the English and Welsh coasts, and Viking bands extended their influence and culture into the surrounding country-side. They captured portions of Irish land in order to extend their city-states, they made alliances with local Irish chieftains, and they married Irish women. In time, a new line emerged amongst the Irish people — the Gael-Goidl (the foreign Gaels), who were a cultural hybrid of Norse and Irish influences.

Undoubtedly some of the Norse belief systems passed into the common Irish cultural stream through this new stratum of society, and with them, legends of dwarves and diminutive men may also have been incorporated into the Irish folk-tapestry. Such tales may have mingled with dimly remembered stories of aboriginal dwarf-communities whom the Celts had encountered, either on their arrival in Ireland or on their journey there. The two stereotypes may well have fused to create a small, low-set man, a custodian of ancient lore and traditions, skilled in the ways of some craft, who was always tricky and cunning as far as mortals were concerned. Recalling the clinkers of the dwarf ironsmiths' fires, this character was always dirty and dishevelled. He was also invariably disreputable, preferring his own company to that of other sprites. He was, in fact, the archetypal leprechaun.

The leprechaun's origins in folklore are, therefore, complex. As a character, he is a walking contradiction — he is stupid but at the same time crafty and scheming; he is kind and will work for nothing, but at the same time he is grasping and greedy; he is kind and helpful, but at the same time surly and dismissive. How can all these attributes be reconciled?

The answer is that the leprechaun's origins may lie in a multiplicity of folk beliefs. He may have started out as a vague and ill-defined folk memory of some diminutive race that once coexisted with the early Celts. As the stories of the grogoch suggest, the leprechaun's origins may lie partly in Scotland. But they may also lie elsewhere in the Celtic world. In Brittany, for instance, there is still a strong belief in *fées* — tiny creatures who dwell in rocks and gullies. They try to avoid humans as much as they can; however, once again, they are not above playing tricks on or acting maliciously towards humans when their fancy takes them. It may well be that stories concerning them also influenced Irish folk-tales and, concomitantly, the imagery of the leprechaun. These memories may have mingled with the folk beliefs of other peoples, which also contained legends of small

races and solitary dwarves, to create a kind of fairy
stereotype which found its way into the general corpus
of Irish folklore. These, of course, are only speculations,
for any definitive answer concerning the origins of the
leprechaun are lost in the mists of time and myth.

General Appearance

Although the image of the 'wee man' on Irish or Irish-
related products is fairly consistent — a jolly little fellow
all dressed in green (to symbolise the greenness and
lushness of Ireland) — folkloric accounts of the leprechaun
vary greatly.

The first problem is that of size. Some tales describe
him as being extremely small — 'a wee man, no bigger
than a thumbnail,' small enough to hold in the palm of
one's hand. Other stories describe him as being about
the size of a two-year-old child, which places him in an
almost-human category. The size of the sprite frequently
depends upon where he is seen. If he is glimpsed
hidden under hedges or in gullies ('sheughs') or ditches,
then he tends to be much smaller, in order to increase
his powers of concealment. If he lives in a cave, on the
other hand, or in a ruined building, he may be slightly
larger, since concealment is not absolutely necessary.

Whatever his size, however, all accounts agree that
the leprechaun is usually an untidy and dishevelled
being. His clothing, reflecting the rather haphazard
dress of the nineteenth-century Irish peasantry, is not at
all stylish. There is none of the co-ordination of freshly
laundered green clothes that appears in stereotyped
pictures of him. Instead, he will probably wear an old
green (or bottle-blue) dress coat, red breeches buckled
at the knee, thick woollen stockings and a wide-
brimmed hat, generally slightly askew. Sometimes he

will wear an old 'claw-hammer' coat (an old type of formal dress coat which sports a forked tail, typically worn by what was once known as the 'down-at-heel gentry'). If he wears a shirt, it will be dirty and worn, tucked untidily into his broad belt to give him an unkempt appearance. The overall sartorial impression is either that of the 'reduced Catholic former aristocracy' during the late eighteenth and early nineteenth centuries, when leprechaun mythology began to develop in Ireland, or that of the itinerant working classes which proliferated throughout the countryside during the same period — 'not rich enough to be comfortable, nor poor enough to be destitute.'

Occasionally, the leprechaun will wear a red stocking-cap like a nineteenth-century mariner's. This is simply a piece of red material, drawn into a shape very much like a nightcap and crudely stitched together. Invariably, the stitching is very untidy, as the leprechaun has no skill with a needle and thread. The cap is then pulled well down over the ears for added warmth. As a fashion item, some leprechauns will wear an old tricorn hat, set at a jaunty angle. This gives them a slightly 'roguish' air and makes them (they believe) more attractive to human women.

Given that leprechauns often live in damp, cold places, personal insulation is extremely important to them. Consequently, many wear several layers of clothing, as a protection against the chill of their dank habitats. Despite being encumbered with so much clothing, the sprite is still extremely agile and fleet of foot, and the fact that he is wearing several rather heavy coats does not appear to slow him down when he is being pursued by mortals.

Although shoes are reputedly the leprechaun's stock in trade and he is widely regarded (by humans) as the cobbler of the fairy world, his own footwear leaves a great deal to be desired. His shoes are usually badly worn and shabby, scuffed and muddied from long hours of crouching in gullies and drains. According to some traditions, in olden days leprechauns wore iron boots for durability; but, as humans began to spread across the country, they were forced to abandon these, as the clanking and scraping of the metal frequently drew attention to the leprechaun's movements. They must also have been extremely heavy and uncomfortable to wear! Nowadays, the boots are made of a more flexible leather and are ornamented with silver buckles like an eighteenth-century dandy's. Many of these shoes also have slightly exaggerated heels built into them. This is to give the impression of height, because — although they very rarely mention it — leprechauns are extremely sensitive about their height.

Greens and browns are the colours most favoured by leprechauns — although the green is not the sharp Lincoln hue which appears in many artistic representations. These colours are favoured for two reasons. Firstly, they are the colours of concealment. To avoid capture by inquisitive mortals, the leprechaun has to dart through bushes and along muddy tracks, and these hues act as camouflage as he does so. He can therefore pass unseen by mortal eyes. Secondly, the brown shade matches the colour of the sprite's own skin, which is dusky and weather-beaten from so many hours in the open air and sun. All these colours seem to merge to give a kind of invisibility to the sprite as he moves through the undergrowth around his home.

The tints of the clothing are created using home-made dyes. The green and red dyes are extracted from lichens, which the leprechaun usually finds growing near his home, but he is also adept at using many other materials as they come to hand. This gives his clothing a kind of rough-and-ready appearance, and — especially as some leprechauns appear to vary in size at certain times of the year, thus making their clothing seem ill-fitting — it adds to his overall air of dishevelment.

Because leprechauns have a natural aversion to water, few of them wash with any sort of regularity. Furthermore, due to the heavy layers of clothing that some of them wear, they tend to be extremely sweaty, especially in summer. Not being the most hygienic of creatures, they allow the sweat to dry upon their skins, thus creating a personal stench that would make many of the strongest mortals flinch.

This personal odour is greatly exacerbated by the fact that many leprechauns smoke dudeens, foul-smelling clay pipes. Though he very rarely smokes tobacco, the leprechaun usually finds enough leaves and other items to give off a pungent reek. According to one tradition, a certain West Clare leprechaun found dried bird-droppings extremely good for smoking. The smoke of the pipe only adds to his overall pungency and keeps the other, more hygienic fairies away from him.

In some areas, leprechauns refuse to have their hair cut. Consequently they are covered, like grogochs, in long, thick, greasy strands of hair, which stretch half-way down their backs. The lengremen of South Armagh actually use their hair as a covering while they sleep because it is so long. However, in other parts of the country — in Galway and Kerry, for example — the leprechaun's hair seems to grow very slowly. Even so, it looks untidy and often leaves his hat reclining at a rather rakish angle — a fashion anomaly which he seldom bothers to correct. And, like the grogoch's, the leprechaun's hair is full of leaves, twigs and branches from the ditches and sheughs through which he has travelled.

Chapter Two

Habitat and Habits

Habitat

Generally speaking, leprechauns prefer to adapt already existing locations for accommodation purposes rather than to construct new dwellings from scratch. In many cases, they will use portions of extant human habitations — ruined houses, old barns, even fallen church ruins. For example, a ruined church on the tiny Inner Hebridean island of Sanda was said to house one of these sprites, who was to be seen of an evening fishing from the cliffs and watching boats going to and from the Mull of Kintyre.

These church- and monastery-dwelling fairies have their roots in Northern English traditions, where they are known as 'abbey lubbers', mischievous sprites who tormented lazy clergy and reminded lax and greedy monks of their vows of austerity. They also helped themselves to the abbey's finest wines. When the abbeys and monasteries fell into neglect, the abbey lubbers stayed on, frightening away anyone who came near with terrifying shrieks and strange noises.

Leprechauns also made their homes in ruined castles and ancient fortresses. A number of Scottish castles are inhabited by leprechaun-like creatures known as gleistigs. There is some dispute as to whether these entities are male (like the leprechaun) or female, but it is generally agreed that they come from the same stock as the Irish sprite. Gleistigs were supposed to inhabit grand houses and castles, long after the human inhabitants had left.

In his seminal book *The Peat Fire's Flame* (1937), Alasdair Alpin MacGregor mentions a particular gleistig which dwelt on the holy island of Iona. Any shepherd who used the island shielings (shelters) was required to pay the sprite a fee for doing so. He had to take a can of ewe's milk to 'a common spot' known locally as the Gleistig's Rock, and pour it into a long crack in the surface of the stone. Failure to do this would result in some sort of murrain (sickness) falling upon his flock, or in some nasty and mischievous trick being played upon the shepherd himself. No real description of this solitary fairy exists, although it is generally thought of in the same generic terms as the leprechaun and is frequently imagined to be female. Its home was believed to be within the rock, and consequently the stone could never be moved.

Similarly, on Eilean Mor, the major island in the Flannan Isles grouping west of Lewis, shepherds and wildfowlers who stayed on the island overnight had to perform a certain ritual so that a fairy force there would not torment them. According to Mary Harman, in her book on St Kilda — *An Isle Called Hirte* (1997) — visitors to Eilean Mor had to make a circuit of the ruined chapel there on their knees, in the direction of the rising sun, praying all the while. Undoubtedly this was to protect them from a supernatural fairy-creature who was said to have made his abode there and who had driven off the monks who originally built the holy site. Indeed, local shepherds who worked for MacLeod of Lewis (who owned the islands) frequently spoke of the unnatural creature which dwelt on Eilean Mor; they referred to the island as 'the other country'. In 1900, three keepers vanished from the newly constructed lighthouse there — a mystery which has never been solved — and widely believed folklore recounts that they were carried off by the fairy in the middle of a storm. The creature is not known to have any particular habitation on the small island, but it is believed to dwell in the ruins of the old church.

In his *Superstitions of the Highlands and Islands of Scotland* (1901), the Reverend J.G. Campbell recounts how solitary, leprechaun-like creatures also inhabit ruined castles. He cites Dunstaffinge Castle, formerly the residence of Scottish kings, as the habitation of a stunted, rather ugly fairy-creature which he describes as being female — an ell-maid. She is particularly attentive to those who stay at the castle, mischievously stripping their beds or making off with items of clothing, which are then found in some other part of the building. These, of course, are also favourite leprechaun tricks.

Other such fairies are said to reside in ruined castles and churches along the Irish coast. An old story from County Limerick recounts how Irish fishermen who passed by such ruins frequently had to share their catches with the creatures, for fear of having something happen to them on the way home:

I used to hear that there was an old castle one time near Killgobban and that its stones were badly tumbled [the place lay in ruins]. A fairy had come to lodge in the place and was a great torment to all the people that lived round about. There was a fisherman called

Niall Hogan who lived quite close to the place, and he used to fish every day from the rocks below the headland on which the fallen castle stood. The road down to and up from these rocks always led him past the castle, and if he had a particularly good day at the fishing, the fairy would always call out to him whenever he passed by, 'Give us a wee one, Niall!' And he would have to leave a fish beside a big stone for the fairy to lift.

He noticed that the oftener he acceded to the fairy's requests, the more frequent and troublesome it became, sometimes demanding two or three fishes from the day's catch. He never saw the fairy, but he knew that it was there, and he could never tell whether it was male or female, for the voice sounded of both genders. The local people said that it was a leprechaun and that he should pay it no heed, but Niall wasn't so sure. It was better, he said, to give it the fish, in case some harm should befall him or the fish from the sea should suddenly dry up and leave him with nothing. So he left as many fish as the fairy asked for. Sometimes it pestered him so much on his way home from fishing that, by the time he had reached his own front door, he had scarcely a single fish left.

At last, a local farmer decided to destroy the old castle entirely — there's not a trace of it to be seen now — and the fairy's demands stopped. Niall was left in peace.

Old churches, too, were considered to be the dwelling-places of leprechauns. In many tales concerning the sprites, the consecrated ground upon which such buildings stood did not seem to bother them. At the site of an ancient monastery in South Armagh, reputedly dedicated to an obscure saint named MacCuagh, a leprechaun was supposed to have taken up his abode.

'You could see him only on very bright days when the sun fell a certain way across the fields,' said Minnie Murphy, a storyteller from Mullaghban in County Armagh. 'And he would appear like a shadow, coming and going among the rays of sunlight just beyond the corner of your eye. If you looked at him directly, he was gone away among the bushes, quick as a thrush. I never saw him myself, but I was told that he was a little fellow, not any bigger than a child, and that you could never really see what he looked like. And he would call out to you sometimes, but his voice would always be like the cry of a bird away in the meadows. He spoke in an old, old language, so that you would never really understand what he was saying. And you could never really get a good look at him. But he was there, all right, even though the place was supposed to be holy ground and blessed by Saint MacCuagh himself. He hasn't been seen nor heard for a long while now. I suppose the people stopped believing in him and he went away.'

In County Tipperary, near Clonmel, a leprechaun is supposed to guard a largely disused well which is on the site of a former church. In this respect, he took over the function of the ancient Celtic clergy, who used to protect the well as a holy place. It was reputedly a healing well, and the priest used to live close by it in a little house, collecting donations from the pilgrims who came to be cured. When the church was abandoned, the leprechaun seems to have taken over the role of the clergy. A token would be left beside the well for the little fellow before the pilgrim used the waters. If this was not done, then the cure would be ineffective or might only last for a short time. Probably the leprechaun was a memory of some ancient well-spirit, dating back to pagan times.

Leprechauns sometimes make their abodes in artefacts

associated with humans, as well as in ruined dwellings. For example, they might live in abandoned beehives, in the eaves of barns, in old boxes or even in discarded kettles.

More usually, however, they choose to live in the open, and there is a good reason for this. Being a sprite of the earth, the leprechaun possesses a magical power over natural things, and it is easy for him, with a little bit of 'fairy glamour' (false imagery created through magic), to make his abode blend in with the existing landscape. Indeed, leprechauns are so skilled at creating illusions that a human might be standing only a few feet away from such a fairy dwelling and not be aware of its existence.

As has already been mentioned in relation to the grogoch, some leprechauns choose to live in places where large standing stones provide some protection against the elements. This firmly establishes the fairy's connection with pagan sites. They may also live in the depths of clumps of thorn-bushes or amid the roots of isolated trees, recalling the notion of tree-worship in the pre-Christian era. This is why such growths are better left undisturbed by farmers or land-developers.

Because of these pagan connotations, many leprechauns are believed to construct their dwellings near the ancient mounds, tumuli, raths and earthen forts that were raised by long-vanished peoples. Often, such places were also deemed to be the homes of the fairy folk themselves — the Macara Shee or trooping fairies — and were to be strenuously avoided. Like the fairy palaces within the raths or forts, the leprechauns' houses — so subtly blended into the landscape as to be undetectable — remained invisible to the naked human eye and might only be seen if the person concerned had had his or her eyes anointed with a special fairy potion, or was carrying a special four-leafed shamrock or clover.

Places scattered across the fields where grass refused to grow were sometimes also considered to indicate leprechauns' houses. The building itself was believed to be invisible, but the telltale grassless patch gave away its location. However, mortals had to be careful not to inadvertently step on such areas when crossing fields or laneways, as doing so would place the traveller within the leprechaun's power. The fairy would then lead the unfortunate mortal astray, and he or she would wander for hours in a lost or dazed condition before being released from the enchantment. The only release from such a spell was to turn one's coat inside out and repeat the Lord's Prayer. Only then would the fairy influence of the place be lifted.

Still other leprechauns chose dry caves or burrows for their homes. These are frequently described as being what we might call 'taller' fairies — 'about the height of a child of two or three' — but still much smaller than mortals.

In 1831, a labourer who was walking along the seashore near Uig, on the Isle of Lewis, noticed that some very bad weather had washed away a large sandbank, exposing the entrance to a small, low cave. Curiosity got the better of him; he poked his head into the opening and saw, to his amazement, a large beehive-shaped dwelling made out of clay, deep in the interior of the cave. Thinking that there might be treasure in it, left over from the Viking occupation of the island, he smashed a section of it open.

Suddenly the air was filled with a kind of angry crying, like a thousand voices mixed with the low drone of bees. Terrified that he had destroyed part of a leprechaun's or brownie's habitation, the labourer dropped his implements and ran.

When he returned home, his wife, who was made of much sterner stuff than he, made him go back and investigate further. Peering into the queer structure, he found a number of objects which he originally thought to be Little People. These were in fact a full set of ninety-three chess-pieces, exquisitely carved from walrus ivory. They are now on display in the British Museum as the Lewis chessmen (reproductions of them are on sale everywhere), and historians have dated them to the eleventh or twelfth century.

Some of the Lewis Islanders, however, tell a different story. These chessmen are the work of a fairy sculptor who once dwelt on the island — a leprechaun-like figure who dwelt alone amongst the sand-dunes. And who is to say that this is not the truth of it?

The smaller types of leprechaun most often live in gullies or sheughs, particularly where the hedges have grown down to give protection. It is particularly difficult to investigate these places, for the leprechaun will pick the most inaccessible area of the drain in which to establish his house, and so the investigator will be torn and mauled by brambles and thorns in trying to see the leprechaun-dwelling and will probably end up not seeing it at all.

A sure signal that a leprechaun is concealed some-where along a gully or drain is said to be the tapping sound which he makes whilst working at a pair of brogues or other shoes. If a mortal coming too close to his house disturbs the leprechaun, he will abandon the shoe and scamper back into the concealment of his abode. Consequently, a small number of storytellers are able to produce discarded shoes which leprechauns have left behind. The most famous of these was the folklorist W.J. Fitzpatrick, who lived in the Mourne Mountains of County Down in the early part of the twentieth century. A photograph of a discarded fairy shoe that he kept in his possession was printed in the *Mourne Observer* in the 1950s, but since the photo was taken, the shoe has mysteriously disappeared.

Although leprechauns' houses are often hard to find, sometimes mortals will stumble upon them by accident. If this should occur, the mortal must never, under any circumstances, accept hospitality from the sprite, as severe repercussions are bound to ensue. The following story comes from the Bog of Allen, in the south-east midlands, and serves as a warning of such consequences:

There was a girl one time had gone to a fair with a young man on whom she was very sweet. On the way home, they fell out — as lovers will sometimes do — and, in a fit of temper, she jumped down from the ass-cart that he was driving and stormed off along the road. He, being in an equally bad temper, drove on home without her, shouting that a good walk would do her no harm and would serve to cool her passion and stay her bad tongue.

The thing was that she had jumped from the cart in the middle of a bog, and was forced to walk along long and lonely roads without ever meeting a single person. Ah, but there's a warning to us all there, not to be so hasty in our words and actions!

Soon night was coming down upon her and she was nowhere near her home. There was a smurr [a slight drizzle] of rain on the wind as well, and, having no head-covering and fearing a bit of a storm, she looked around for some sort of shelter. Away out in the bog, she saw the light of a window, and she thought that she might go there and ask for a wee bit of shelter for the night. Then she could set out for home again in the morning.

There was only a peat road leading into the bog towards the light, and it was badly grown about with reeds and rushes and spiky bushes. All the same, the girl forced her way on towards the light, and just as the sun was going down, she came upon a little house of sods built in the very heart of the bog, with a bit of an old haw-lantern in its window. And sitting in front of its open door on a three-legged stool was a wee man, no bigger than a two-year-old child, smoking an old dudeen in the last of the evening. Beside him on the ground lay an old fiddle and bow. He was warming himself in front of a small fire that he had lit in front of his doorway.

He looked up at her as she came out of the dark, and she saw that his skin was tanned and weather-beaten and that his hair and beard were as black as coal. But it was his eyes, which were quick and intelligent, that took her interest.

She told him that she was a traveller who was a long way from home, and that she would be grateful if he would let her lie by his fire for the night and share his family's meal.

The little man looked at her queerly. 'I live here alone,' says he, with a queer accent in his tone that reminded her of Old Irish. 'But you are welcome to share what I have. I must tell you that I am a bit of a musician, and that on nights such as this, my neighbours, who also live in this bog, will gather here for a bit of a céilí. But you are welcome to join in with us if you have a mind to, for there will not be much sleeping done this night.'

Now the girl was always ready for a céilí, and she readily agreed. The little old man beckoned her into the house, and when she got into the place, she found out just how low it was. She could barely stand up in it, and there appeared to be no furniture about it at all — just a few old seats and a table. The floor had been swept quite clean, though, as if ready for some merriment.

The man produced an old jug of poteen and the

two of them went outside to enjoy the night. Gradually, other people began to come out of the twilight, coming from different directions across the bog. Not one of them was any bigger than a child, although they all appeared to be very old, and the girl noticed that she was the only woman amongst them all. Every one of them was a little old man.

Her host lifted his fiddle and began a merry tune, and soon the céilí was in full swing, away in that remote and lonely place. The girl so enjoyed the music that she got up to dance, and soon she was leaping with the best of them around the fire at the doorway of the small house.

She danced and danced until it seemed that she would never stop; as soon as she had finished dancing with one of the small men, another would step up to take his place. And every time she paused for breath, someone would come forward with a cup of poteen for her. She would gulp it down and dance some more. She danced until her feet were numb and she was exhausted — so exhausted that she collapsed in a heap, just in front of the doorway of the house of sods.

She awoke in the middle of the bog, with nobody next nor near her. Of the house, the fire and the noisy company, there was no sign. She lay with her head almost in a bog-hole and a fearsome pain in her feet. When she looked down, she saw that they were covered in blood. Indeed, she had danced so much that her feet were raw and she had almost danced her toes off. It was only then that she realised that she had been dancing all night with the leprechauns of the bog, those tireless dancers who fade away on the wind as soon as the sun is up.

Getting up, she limped back to the road and eventually made her way home. When she came

near her own house, she began to notice how things
had changed. On the road, near to her own gate, she
met a couple of people coming down towards her.
She looked at them and they at her, but neither
recognised the other. And the houses were different,
too — where there should have been thatch, there
was now slate, and where the walls should have
been whitewashed with lime, they were now dashed
with pebbles. And she passed houses by the roadside
that she never remembered seeing before. It was all
very strange. The people working in the fields
seemed different, too. There were young people that
she should have known but didn't recognise, and the
fields which had been boggy and rushy when she had
left that morning were now flat and cultivated, with
cattle grazing in them or crops growing there.

At length she came to her own gateway, and right
glad she was to see it, for her poor feet were in
agony. She hobbled up to the door, but as she did so,
a strange woman came to the door and asked her
what she wanted.

'I want to come into my own house!' said the girl
rather angrily.

The woman just looked at her in astonishment. 'I
don't know who you are,' she said, with a stiff tone
in her voice, 'nor what you think you're doing, but
this is not your house!' She said it with such finality
that the girl knew she wasn't lying. 'Now get away from
my door, old woman, and be about your business.'

The girl looked at her, aghast. Who was this
cheeky besom who referred to her as an 'old
woman'? The woman at the door looked old enough
to be her mother!

'This is indeed my house!' she told her. 'At least,
it was when I left here this morning. And who are
you, anyway, to come claiming it for your own?'

The woman gave her a look of distaste. 'I have lived here with my husband these last twenty years,' she told the astonished girl. 'And before me it was a family named Mulligan, who moved away to Ballina in the County Mayo. And long before that it was a family named Cosendine....'

The girl gasped. 'But that's my name!' she told the strange woman. 'I'm Kate Cosendine.'

The woman looked at her curiously for a moment, then made the sign of the Cross in the air above her head. 'Lord help me!' she cried, stepping back into the cottage. 'You're Kitty Cosendine that vanished all those years ago, on her way home from the fair with Dan Sullivan. I mind my grandmother telling me about it, for it all happened when she was a child herself.'

Kitty sat down on the edge of the doorstep, a great weariness suddenly overcoming her.

'Look at yourself, woman!' And she fetched a mirror for Kitty to see herself.

What she saw looking back at her was the face of an old, old woman, dirty like a beggar-hag, with straggly graying hair and the lines of great age all across her withered skin. Gone was the young girl who had left home all those years ago — years that had passed in a single night's dancing with the leprechauns out in the bog.

The woman drove her away from her door, and for most of the day she wandered the roads, hearing bits of stories about herself — for the legend of Kitty Cosendine was well-known in the locality. It appeared that Dan Sullivan had waited for her for many years but had eventually married another girl. His grandchildren still lived nearby. Her family had fallen on hard times and had been forced to move on, and now no trace of them remained in the countryside.

There was nowhere for Kitty to go and no one to take her in. Her feet ached, but she had to keep walking; she had no rest at all.

As evening drew on, she approached the church. Dragging herself up the steps, she peered in through the door. A service was in progress and the priest was in the very act of elevating the Host. And as he called God's blessing on all present, Kitty Cosendine fell away to dust with a final sigh. She had found her rest at last.

But her story is a warning to one and all against accepting the hospitality of the leprechauns, or of any other fairy-creature. Their ways are not our ways; neither is their time like ours. Those who sit by the fires of the Sídhe may find that their time has already passed without them realising it.

It was not always easy to recognise fairy houses, and humans were wont to stumble upon them by accident. Bogs and mosses throughout the countryside were frequently the habitation of leprechauns, harking back to an old meaning of the name — 'rushy man'. Their huts were either of peats cut from the bog itself, or of rushes and grass tied into intricate designs. In the evening, the voices of the leprechauns could be heard crying from their secret houses among the rushes, the sounds high and shrill like those of waterfowl. Cynics may very well say that these are no more than the cries of birds nesting in the bogs, but the wise man is not always so dismissive. It would be folly, however, to follow such cries in order to see the leprechaun: the sounds might lead you into the most dangerous part of the swamp, and you might never find your way out again, or might sink into the mud without a trace. Hunting leprechauns in such terrain is a dangerous business indeed!

Drink

The leprechaun is usually described as a 'fairy shoe-maker', but, as we shall see later, this is not always true. Many leprechauns do not need to work, as they often know the whereabouts of ancient treasure which can keep them in the manner to which they wish to become accustomed. Some of them do not work at all. And perhaps it is just as well, for most leprechauns have an inherent weakness: they are all exceptionally fond of strong drink, particularly poteen.

To say that illicit spirits are an integral part of leprechaun culture would be something of an under-statement. Indeed, much of the leprechaun's day revolves around the manufacture and consumption of the same. The leprechaun constitution must be an extremely sturdy one, for not only does the creature consume staggering amounts of liquor (enough to render several battalions of strong mortal men senseless), but the concoction which he drinks is so impure that it would be positively fatal to mortals. As has already been stated, hygiene is not a paramount consideration in the leprechaun's world, and this lack of cleanliness is often evident in the fairy's distilling process.

The leprechaun will use almost any abandoned mortal domestic utensil as a basis for his 'still' — an old pot, an earthen jar, a kettle coated in rust. The impurities which the raw spirit might absorb from these vessels appears to be of little concern to him, as long as the end result can be drunk. He will distil his spirit from all sorts of available rubbish — old potato peelings, bits of old turnip, carrots, and so on — as well as from the conventional barley grain.

In most cases, leprechauns do not distil for profit (in other words, they do not sell the results of their efforts — although a very few may do so, on occasion); they prepare the majority of their brews for their own consumption. Consequently few of them are seen without a quart jug, from which they will take a swig from time to time, somewhere nearby.

The sprite's habitation of ruined castles and houses adds to the availability of distilling space, and old cupboards or niches can quickly be converted into areas in which spirit-production can easily take place. As well as manufacturing spirits, the leprechaun is also extremely adept at preparing wines, ales and beers, which he drinks with consummate gusto. Despite the large quantities of liquor that he imbibes, and despite the fact that he is often extremely tipsy, the leprechaun is seldom so drunk that he can be easily caught by a mortal hunter or by a scavenging animal or bird. Even in an inebriated state, he can still move with surprising speed and alacrity.

Leprechauns also enjoy drink which has been spilled from human glasses. Some will sit invisibly in public houses, trying to jog the elbows of the drinkers so that they will spill a sup of stout or a small measure of whiskey for the leprechaun's convenience. If a drop is spilled, it is customary to say, 'Here's a drop for you, little fellow,' to ensure good luck on the coming day. If it is cleaned up too hastily (that is, before the leprechaun can sup it up), misfortune may descend not only upon the individual drinker but upon the licensed establishment as well.

The sprites will also hang around the doorways of houses in the hope that some drink will accidentally be spilled inside. This has a number of grave dangers for them. The foremost of these is that the owner of the house may throw out water at the end of the day, drenching the little fellow as he waits invisibly in the evening light. If this happens, the leprechaun is, understandably, not best pleased, and he may take some form of revenge against the household concerned. It is therefore prudent to shout a warning before throwing water out into the dusk. A common warning might be *'Hugitas, ugitas, uisce salach!'* ('Away, away, dirty water!') Upon hearing this, all fairy-creatures know to withdraw from the immediate vicinity of the door for fear of being splashed.

Leprechauns are not terribly partial to other human drinks such as tea or coffee, although they will sample a cup if there is nothing else available. It is thought that the caffeine in both beverages will bring the fairy out in itchy welts and blotches, similar to hives in a human being, and will leave him feeling uncomfortable. If all else fails, the leprechaun will drink spring water (but not tap water), although he will do so with an ill grace, muttering and complaining all the while. Leprechauns and water are not terribly compatible. He will do his best to avoid fizzy drinks such as lemonade, as these will make him bloated and queasy. It is therefore better for him to stick to supping poteen — the drink that he knows best.

Food

Generally speaking, leprechauns will eat roughly the same food as humans. The few accounts that we have of fairy food suggest that it is not terribly substantial or filling, and whilst it may suit the trooping fairies — who are always very fussy about their figures — it is hardly fit for a hungry leprechaun who has no such worries. However, his tastes are very plain, and he will not eat sweet biscuits or fancy side dishes, simply because he does not like them. Nor will he touch processed food, so tins of beans, peas or pasta in tomato sauce are practically poison to him. Being a traditionalist, he is wary of any sort of foreign food. Curries, kebabs and even Chinese food are all anathema to him, although a few of the sprites have been known to eat the topping off pizza (but only if it is made with fresh tomatoes and cheese!) Traditionally speaking, the leprechaun is known to consume large quantities of potatoes, washed down with either poteen or sweet milk. He is also partial to the occasional side of beef or chicken leg, when he can get them, and he has been known to raid the larders of sleeping mortals in order to obtain them.

Generally, the leprechaun contents himself with whatever crumbs and scraps he can take from the tables of humans. If a morsel of food falls to the ground, it immediately becomes his property and should not be retrieved. In certain parts of Ireland − for example, Connemara − crusts of bread, and other pieces of food that had been discarded or dropped, were traditionally placed on a convenient window-ledge as a kind of 'offering' to the leprechauns.

There are, however, a number of delicacies which are specific to leprechauns, and are detrimental to mortals. For example, leprechauns, like many other fairies, find fungi of varying types particularly tasty. Toadstools, in particular, are often the basis of their nourishing broths (nourishing to them, that is, since most humans would find such a concoction extremely poisonous). And amongst their most famous comestibles is the so-called 'fairy butter', a soft, cheese-like fungus which grows on the boles of very old trees. This is the central ingredient in most fairy cookery − particularly baking. On no account should a human eat this mould, for it will be found to be at best almost tasteless, at worst utterly poisonous. In the fairy world, however, this butter is used both as a condiment and as a relish, and leprechauns keep great stores of it near to their dwellings − so, if a mortal comes across the fungus growing at the base of a tree, there is sure to be a leprechaun's house somewhere close by.

The roots of the silverweed, too, are especially sought after by the little men. They are used as the basis of many soups and stews, which the sprites prepare in small iron pots. It is thought that these roots were once also the staple food of Irish mortals, who gave up eating them as soon as potatoes were imported from the New World. Heather is also used in leprechaun cuisine, to thicken stews and gravies on the sprite's table; it can also be brewed into a fine beer which can be drunk along with the meal. The secret of making heather beer was once known to all men, but over the years it was forgotten, and it is now one of the most famous 'lost arts' of Ireland. It was certainly still known to two old Viking brothers who lived in Donegal in the mid-twelfth century, but upon their deaths it was forgotten and so lost. Now, only the leprechauns remember the recipe. Heather stems are sometimes also served as sweetmeats at the end of a meal — a kind of *digestif* for cleansing both the palate and the teeth.

Although the leprechaun finds food pleasant to eat, however, it is not essential to him. As long as he eats once in a while, he can go for days without partaking of any such nourishment. Poteen is more essential to him than a staple diet!

Music

Like all fairies, leprechauns have a great love of music and are often skilled musicians. Because they have such phenomenal memories, they can carry tunes in their heads long after mortals have forgotten them. As a result, the leprechauns can both remember and play — note for note — ancient folk-tunes which are no longer available to most mortal musicians. Many a fiddler or pipe-player, and many a harper too, has heard strange and beautiful melodies wafting on the morning or the evening breeze, from bogs and hollows where leprechauns are said to dwell. Rory Dall O'Cahan, the composer credited with one of the most famous of all Irish melodies — 'The Londonderry Air', better known as 'Danny Boy' — reputedly heard it being played upon a leprechaun's harp along the marshy banks of the Roe River in North Derry. He wrote it down, and its beauty has entranced Irish people (and many others) ever since. It is said to be one of the very few tunes which can reduce a true Irishman to tears when he hears it.

Because of the great beauty and antiquity of their melodies, leprechauns are said to guard them rather strictly. Woe betide the musician who writes down a fairy tune and passes it off as his own, for the 'wee people' will be sure to have their revenge upon such an upstart! An old and frequently repeated tale from the West of Ireland illustrates this point:

There was a piper in Mayo one time — one of the O'Malleys — who was very much in demand for the skill of his playing and for the sweetness of his tunes. He lived in a little house near the coast, with only his dog for company, for he was a solitary man who liked only his own company for most of the time.

One evening, he had been playing at a céilí in Castlebar and the festivities had gone on throughout the night. So it was early in the morning that he was making his way home. He had only gone a couple of miles from the céilí-house when he chanced on a little glen close by the roadside. I won't tell you where it is, for it is a fairy place and the leprechauns can often be seen there yet, gambolling and sporting, even at midday.

Well, as the Piper O'Malley passed by this glen, he heard music drifting up into the morning air from the hollow below. He ventured down to take a closer look, his little dog slinking down through the bushes behind him. A leprechaun was sitting on a large rock in the middle of a stream, playing on a set of ancient pipes, and the melody that he played was so beautiful that it would have broken your heart to hear it.

Now, O'Malley had a great ear for the notes and a great memory for the music, and he was able to remember the tune as it floated around him on the breeze. He stole back to the road and made his way home, keeping the music in his head all the while.

From that day onwards, he included the fairy tune amongst those that he played, and he always passed it off as his own. He never told anyone that he'd heard it from a leprechaun. Everyone who heard it thought that it was a most beautiful melody and declared that O'Malley was little short of a genius for having composed (as they thought) such a delicate air. But fairy tunes are not to be trifled with or to be claimed by mortals as their own.

Some time after, O'Malley was playing at a céilí on the wild Mayo coast. He played the fairy air several times, and the people were well satisfied. Again, it was early in the morning when he set out for home, with his dog at his heels. As they were passing through a particularly remote part of the coast, O'Malley suddenly heard yet another tune being played on the pipes, even more beautiful than the first that he'd heard. He made his way down to see who was playing, with his dog close behind him.

The music seemed to be coming from a large cave in the cliff-face a little way below him. He looked around for a way down, and, sure enough, there was a little gravel path leading downwards to the very mouth of the cavern. Without hesitating, the Piper O'Malley scrambled down, his mouth fairly watering at the thought of stealing another melody from the fairies.

However, as he stood at the mouth of the cave, the music suddenly seemed less distinct and farther away. In order to hear it better, the Piper stepped into the cave, going farther and farther into its depths. His dog followed, close at his heels.

That was the last that anyone saw of the Piper O'Malley, although his dog did appear some time later, shaking with fear, out of a burrow about two or three miles away. But no trace of his master has been found, even to this day.

But if you should venture along the Mayo coastline at certain times of the year, and if you should happen to be passing a place where there are caves, you may hear the strains of music coming from the depths of one of them. It is a lonely, eerie sound, and so beautiful that it will break your heart to hear it. People will tell you that it is the music of the Piper O'Malley, held as a prisoner in the Otherworld by the leprechauns whose tune he stole, and that the music contains the strains of his longing to get back to the mortal realm. Of course, there are those who will tell you that there is nothing to it — that it is only the sound of the wind in the caves — but I'll wager that there are few of them who will venture deep into these caverns to investigate. And these same people will stay well away from the rugged and lonely Mayo coastline at certain times of the year. That's the vengeance of the leprechauns, all right — for they disapprove very strongly of people taking their tunes and claiming them for their own. That's the way of it, all right.

As the above story demonstrates, leprechauns are very skilled musicians who can turn their hands to any tune. This skill, they claim, has been handed down to all the fairy kind since the days of the Tuatha de Danann, who came from the East (or the sun, depending on the version of the tale) in a golden mist and brought music, poetry and culture to Ireland. The Tuatha de Danann also brought the Irish harp, which is the simplest-seeming of all musical instruments and yet is one of the hardest to play. The Gaels took over the playing of the harp and used it at great banquets and feasts, and the leprechauns mimic this ability and will sometimes play the harp at their own gatherings. However, they can turn their hands to almost any instrument, but greatly favour the fiddle or the Irish pipes.

Many of the old songs and tunes which they play are said to come from earliest times — from the period of the Tuatha de Danann themselves. This is not always true, for leprechauns remember old mortal melodies which people have long forgotten and can often play them note for note, passing them off as mystical fairy tunes. The music of the Tuatha de Danann is more abstract than this; it is quite ethereal and is not really suited to any human instrument except the harp.

One must always be extremely careful when listening to leprechaun music, especially the livelier jigs and reels. The sprite may include some magic within the tune, and, like the girl in the story told earlier, the listener may find it impossible to resist dancing. Seeing that he has the dancer in his power, the leprechaun will increase the speed and tempo of the tune, making his captive leap and gambol faster and faster in time with the music. This he does for spite and mischief, and some people have been known to die from exhaustion after performing a 'leprechaun's reel'.

The greatest leprechaun harpers and pipers are

generally said to come from the Munster area, while the best of the fiddle-players and lyricists are believed to reside in Ulster. It is said that leprechaun tunes have no lyrics until they drift into Ulster, and that their poems have no melody until they come further south. This, of course, is not strictly true, but serves as a 'rule of thumb'.

In order to exchange melodies, poems and lyrics, leprechauns from all over Ireland meet at gatherings and fairs that take place at certain times of the year. Here, they play one another the latest melodies which they have acquired, and in this way the tunes pass into the general fairy repertoire.

Festivals and Céilís

There is nothing the leprechaun likes more than a good céilí, since these are nothing more than excuses for intemperate drinking and merrymaking. Because of his solitary nature, he does not get the opportunity for either very often, so he has to make the most of such gatherings when and as they come along.

There are, however, a number of fixed dates in the leprechaun's social calendar.

The two most important gatherings are at May Eve and at Hallowe'en. These are, of course, general fairy festivals, when the gates of the raths and mounds of the Sídhe are thrown open and the Macara Shee (the fairy cavalcade) takes to the road on its progress through the countryside. These festivals divide the year into two halves — light and dark, warm and cool — and provide opportunities for the fairies to show their finery. The leprechaun, having no such finery to show, turns his hand to other things; it is usually at these times of the year that he moves house (if he has a mind to) or else makes repairs to his dwelling. These festivals are also opportunities for him to erect new stills for his illegal spirits, or to seek out new places where such stills can be situated.

May Eve (30 April–1 May) marks the start of the summer, which is a celebration of the return to full strength and of optimism regarding growing things and new life. The festival also looks forward to the year's harvest, and so it had great significance for our ancient agricultural ancestors. It is at this time that the leprechaun makes the most of his illicit spirits, which he stores away for the coming year at various locations scattered across the countryside. There are gatherings in various parts of the country, as leprechauns arrive to sample one another's batches of poteen, and the mood is incredibly drunken and lively.

Hallowe'en (31 October), on the other hand, is a gloomy and sombre time, when one's thoughts are reflective and are focused on the year which is almost past. Once again, the Macara Shee troop around the countryside, but this time there is an added element to their cavalcade. This is the time when the veil between the mortal world and the Otherworld is at its most fragile, and many unsettling creatures often cross from the Beyond into our own world to walk abroad. It is the time when the banshee cries her wailing cry, signifying death in the year to come; and the pouka gallops along the ill-lit lanes, terrifying animals, curdling the milk in the udders of the cows and preventing the hens from laying. It is also a time when the shrouded, unquiet dead roam the highways and byways of the land.

The leprechaun is not greatly bothered by the banshee or the pouka, or even by the wandering ghosts; he simply keeps out of their way. Besides, he has a number of tricks of his own to play. It is at this time of the year that he is at his most mischievous, and he celebrates the fact by turning the farmer's livestock out of the fields and onto the road; by taking farm gates off their hinges; by causing draughts in the chimney, so that smoke blows down into the kitchen; and by a hundred other pranks. Sometimes, at Hallowe'en, leprechauns will gather together (although not in such great numbers as at May Eve) in order to play their pranks, and will become very intoxicated, thus adding to their mischief. Small feasts, composed of hazelnuts, apples and fairy butter, are consumed at such revelries, and locally distilled poteen, suitably aged, is quaffed with some gusto.

Besides these two great festivals (which are, of course, as important to mortals as they are to the fairy folk), there are other times during the year when the leprechauns will come together to make merry. The first of these is St Brigid's Day (1 February). Although Brigid is the foremost female Christian saint in Ireland, tradition tells us that before her conversion she was a *draoi-ban* (a female druid or pagan priestess), and that she was always a friend to the Little People. Besides, the date of her celebration coincides with the end of winter, the lengthening of the days and the promise of longer evenings; it became known to the Church as Candlemas (the onset of longer evenings is reflected in the old maxim, 'On Candlemas Day throw a candle away'). Before Christianity took it over, however, this was celebrated as a pagan festival, and so the leprechauns (who can well remember the ancient festival) will make merry in celebration of the increased daylight and the formerly pagan saint.

Another time when leprechauns gather together is upon St Patrick's Day (17 March). Although the patron saint of Ireland is not well-regarded amongst the fairy kind (he tricked them out of part of their lands by subtle argument), his feast was at one time celebrated by mortals the length and breadth of Ireland; much of the festivity involved strong liquor, and since large amounts of it tended to be spilled (in ceremonies such as 'drowning the shamrock'), leprechauns took it as a time of festivity as well, catching all the food and drink which fell from human tables and claiming it for their own.

The ancient Celtic feast of Lughnasadh (31 July–1 August), also known as Lammas, is also a festive date in the leprechaun's calendar, albeit a relatively minor one. Strictly speaking, this is a festival for witches — one of darkness and ill omen. In Kerry, the second week of August was at one time known as the *Lughna Dubh* (the dark Lugh festival); it signalled a turn towards darker days and a time when the forces of evil and cold might begin to flex their muscles once again. It was one of the great Sabbats of the witch's year, and as such had little to do with the fairies. Nevertheless, leprechauns still observe it as a kind of minor festival, perhaps to prepare themselves for the dark days of winter or to signal the approaching end of summer. Festivities and merriment are kept to a minimum, and food for the feast consists mainly of old potatoes and kale or cabbage tops, washed down by the invariable plentiful supply of poteen.

Only one other feast-day is observed by the sprites. This is the great festival of Yule (25 December). This is not a time for merriment, because it is the birthday of Our Lord, when all work and play must cease and a period of pious reflection should be observed. Not being Christians, the leprechauns might claim that they are not bound by this day; and yet, like all other fairies, they observe it. Indeed, God compels them to do so: all living things, natural and supernatural, must celebrate the holy time. And during this time, the leprechaun must be completely abstemious, not touching liquor at all. In an act of defiance, many leprechauns spend the day counting their hoards of treasure and gold, in preparation for the coming year. As soon as St Stephen's Day (Boxing Day) comes round, they are back to their pranks and drinking again.

There is one other festival which, although not a feast-day, is specific to leprechauns. This is the Beltane Fair of Uisnech, held each year in County Westmeath just before May Day — usually around 28 or 29 April. Leprechauns travel to this fair from all over Ireland. They come to exchange tunes, riddles, stories and songs, and to show off their prowess at brewing and distilling and at sports and music. This is also the arena in which disputes can be settled and alliances made. Goods are also sold at the fair — usually home-made foods, shoes, and articles which have been stolen from humans.

The event usually runs for several days, culminating in the May Day celebrations. According to some accounts, however, in 1846 and 1847, the event had to be delayed because of the Irish Potato Famine and difficulties in travelling; and on one famous occasion, in 1901, the celebrants became so intoxicated that the fair was unable to continue because no one was sober enough! Such instances, however, are extremely rare. A few mortals have been permitted to witness this occasion, but it is said that those who do invariably forget everything that they have seen within two or three days.

Although a solitary creature by nature, then, the leprechaun certainly knows how to party — and he will take every opportunity to do so! This means he will break into houses and drink from any container of strong liquor which he may find. From time to time, he will become extremely noisy and boisterous. If approached when in this condition, he will become extremely aggressive and abusive; so it is best to leave him to his own devices. Although some folklorists argue that this is the best time to capture him — while he is in an intoxicated state and inside a house — this might not be the case: the leprechaun's reflexes are still extremely quick, and the would-be captor may find that he receives more than he bargained for!

Chapter Three

QUESTIONS OF GENDER, BIRTH AND AGE

Throughout this text, the Irish leprechaun has been referred to as 'he', and there is a good reason for this. Although some folklorists may disagree, there is no substantive evidence for the existence of female leprechauns in Ireland. Niall MacNamara, in his book *The Leprechaun's Companion* (1999), mentions a female of the species but gives little indication as to where she may be found. General opinion, however, noting the inherent solitary nature of the leprechaun, makes no mention of either marriage or courtship. He is portrayed as an isolated bachelor with no female companion or counterpart.

This impression may not be strictly true, for the matter is complicated by the inclusion of the Scottish grogoch in the leprechaun classification. On the Isle of Arran in the Firth of Clyde, grogochs are always considered female. A further complication is added by the definition of a Highland grogoch: this is a witch/wizard who has shape-shifting abilities and may change his/her form and gender at will. In Brittany, the *fées* and *lutins* (little leprechaun-like spirits who either live in the wild or attach themselves to the houses of certain families) are usually considered to be female. However, in Ireland, the leprechaun is believed to be male.

This notion leads to the inevitable question: how do leprechauns reproduce?

This is a problem which has never been satisfactorily answered, for the leprechaun is understandably reluctant to discuss the matter. A creature of utmost secrecy, he cannot be coaxed or cajoled into revealing anything regarding his courtship or reproductive practices.

There are, however, a number of theories as to how leprechauns came to be.

Most leprechauns claim direct descendency from the Tuatha de Danann, who are said to have arrived in Ireland around the third millennium BC. However, there seems to be little basis for this claim. Almost every source describes the Tuatha de Danann as arriving in clouds from the east and settling on a mountain in the west of Ireland, causing a great eclipse of the sun as they did so. They were, say the ancient accounts, an extremely advanced, learned, industrious and exceptionally tall and beautiful people. Some folklorists have compared them to the ancient Greeks. The leprechaun, on the other hand, is small and stunted, rather ugly, and in no way advanced or learned. Therefore, his relationship to the Tuatha de Danann is extremely tenuous.

However, this is not to deny that there may be some sort of connection, for some folklorists have described the leprechaun as an offshoot (or 'by-blow') of the Tuatha de Danann lineage.

It is well-known throughout the Celtic world that fairy women find the process of giving birth extremely difficult. This is probably due to the fact that they give birth extremely infrequently. Having no midwives of their own, they are forced to labour as best they can, or else to employ the services of a human midwife who has a greater knowledge of the birthing process than they. The number of stories of midwives in remote areas of the country being carried off by fairies in order to assist at a birth are to be found all over Ireland, from Donegal to Kerry, and in many other Celtic lands besides.

When the fairy child is first born, it sometimes appears to be a small, wizened, ugly thing which bears little or no resemblance to its often stately and beautiful parents. In most of the folk-tales, it is hustled away before the midwife can see it and seems to disappear from the story. Folklorists have suggested that these stunted and repulsive children form the basis of the leprechaun population. They are cast out of the fairy host, to become either changelings (sickly and complaining fairies who are sometimes left in the place of stolen human children) or the surly, dudeen-smoking sprites of the leprechaun clans. The fact that the leprechaun is, in fact, more or less an outcast from the mainstream fairy world is often cited as a reason for his sullen and anti-social nature as well as for his elusive habits.

All leprechauns, says this theory, are male because the proportion of stunted or deformed male children is much higher in the fairy world than it is in the human world (female fairies are always born as radiant and beautiful creatures with no blemishes whatsoever), and their numbers are added to practically every time a fairy woman gives birth. There is no real evidence for this theory, as none of the stunted fairy offspring have ever been traced and there are no real stories of them beyond their births. However, it remains one of the most plausible accounts of the origins of the leprechaun.

Another theory is that the leprechaun is the product of an illicit union between a fairy and a human. From time to time, according to legend, certain mortals and members of the fairy folk met together as lovers, even though the Church had expressly banned any form of consorting between the two. The product of this union was a small, stunted being — not quite human, but not quite fairy either — who would eventually become a form of dwarf.

Certainly these human-fairy unions were quite common in former times in Ireland, particularly amongst great and heroic men. The Irish hero Dunlaing O'Hartigan, one of the foremost captains in Brian Boru's army at the Battle of Clontarf in 1014, is said to have lain with the fairy woman Aoibheall and had a son by her. Before the battle, Aoibheall appeared in Brian's camp and promised Dunlaing and his mortal sons two hundred years of life if they would put off fighting for one day. She told him that if he did not, he would be slain the next day, and she reminded the captain that they had an infant son — half-human, half-fairy — for whom he was responsible. Being a warrior, O'Hartigan refused, and he and his sons were killed the following day in a fierce battle against the Norsemen. Aoibheall eventually became a banshee — reputedly one of the first in Ireland — on the slopes above Lough Derg. No further mention is made of the half-human child, and some have argued that it might have become a leprechaun-like figure.

A similar story comes from an old folk-tale from Lough Urlaur in County Roscommon. Here, it is said, a fairy came to the door of St Thomas's Church, near the shores of the lough, to plead with her former partner to acknowledge their offspring.

The priest had just begun his homily, and all eyes were fixed upon him, when outside the wind began to rise, like the scream of a thousand voices, and the day seemed to darken slightly beyond the church windows. *The congregation shuffled and muttered amongst themselves uneasily, but the priest continued with his sermon, although his voice seemed to falter slightly.*

Then, above the shriek of the wind, came another voice which drowned out the drone of the priest. It seemed to be the cry of a woman in torment: 'Come out! Come out!' And it named the son of a local gentleman, who sat in the congregation. 'Come out and acknowledge what is truly yours.' The cry was accompanied by a hammering on the church doors which sounded like a roll of thunder.

All heads turned, but the young man sat with a stony face beside his father, looking fixedly towards the altar.

Again the voice cried, 'Come out! I call on you to come from that place and take what is yours!' Again there was the fearful hammering. Even the priest had stopped now, but still nobody made any move.

At last the priest stepped down and walked to the heavy oaken doors of the church, to see who was calling. Throwing the doors wide, he looked out into the dark day.

A beautiful woman stood there, but the holy man could see by her great loveliness and her strange, pale complexion that this was no earthly person. She was one of the Sídhe, who had come down from the rath nearby to beat on the church doors. In the crook of her left arm she held a tiny bundle, and as the priest watched, a tiny arm poked from its coverings and waved in the air.

There was a child in that bundle, thought the astonished cleric. He made the sign of the Cross in the air, to protect against fairy magic. The woman seemed to shrink back slightly, still clutching her bundle tightly.

'*What is it that you want in the House of God?*'
intoned the priest.

The woman drew herself up to her full height,
and the child gurgled in its wrappings. '*I am come
here so that the father of my child can own what
is his,*' said she, '*and so that I can then present my
infant, as the fruit of his loins, for the holy baptism
of the mortal world.*'

The priest stood aghast. '*Surely you know that it
is unlawful in the eyes of our Mother Church for one
of your kind to have relations with the Children of
Adam, for whom Christ died? No Christian man
could have fathered this child.*'

The woman looked at him with tears brimming in
her large and lovely eyes. '*Spoken like a man of the
cloth,*' she replied. '*Spoken without a shred of pity.
Well, priest, let me tell you this. This man*' — and
she named him again — '*is the father of this child —
Christian or no Christian. Let him come forward and
deny it to my face — the face of the woman who
loved him and who loves him yet. And if he does so,
then I must abandon my own child, for that is the
decree of those who dwell within my rath. He will
have not only my own woe upon his shoulders, but
also the woes of the son who has his blood within his
veins. Will he deny the cry of his own human blood?
Let him come to the door and face me now!*'

The priest hesitated. '*It is also against the decree
of our Holy Mother Church for a clergyman to barter
with one of the Sídhe,*' he said at length. '*But you
accuse me of having no pity. I will therefore do as
you ask. I will call the man that you have named to
the door of the church and let him either own or
deny the child. I do it not to satisfy you but for the
sake of the infant in your arms. The Lord Christ
Himself shows mercy to the smallest child — maybe*

even to those of the Sídhe — and who am I to do
otherwise?'

He turned back into the chapel and called out the
young man's name, instructing him to come forward
to the church door. The boy came forward hesitantly,
and there was an air of slyness about him. His father
followed him out of the dark interior of the church
and stood behind him as he faced the fairy woman
and her child. The priest also stood by, his right
hand on the baptismal font which stood just inside
the door.

The boy blinked in the harsh daylight after the
cool gloom of the church, but gave not the slightest
sign that he recognised the fairy.

'I am come to the door of the church,' he said,
glancing at his father out of the corner of his eye.
'What is it that you want with me?'

In reply the fairy gave a kind of low wail and held
out the child, still gurgling merrily in his wrap. 'Only
acknowledge what is yours,' she pleaded, 'so that he
may be baptised in the fashion of the White Christ.
Only then has he any hope of entering Heaven. Oh,
only acknowledge your own son, even if you do not
acknowledge me!'

The boy paused uncertainly. He stole a glance at
his father, who stood almost behind him on his left,
and then at the priest, who stood to his right. Words
paused on his lips. The child laughed and crowed in
the few rays of sunlight that were falling between the
dark clouds overhead.

'Well?' asked the priest. 'Is this truly your child?
Have you been consorting with this woman, against
all the dictates of the Church?'

For a moment there was silence, but at last the
boy spoke.

'How can I acknowledge one of the fairy kind as

my own?' he demanded. 'This has nothing to do with me. It is a trick of the Sídhe, a ploy to get one of their loathly kind to enter Heaven through the sacrament of baptism. Take yourself away, woman, for I know neither yourself nor your brat. I am engaged to be married and would not have you ruin me with your lies. Return to your rath, and trouble me and my family no more!'

He spoke sharply and cruelly, and at his words, the fairy woman gave a terrible howl of despair.

'One thousand years have I lived in the world,' she screamed, 'and in all that time I have seen nothing so heartless as a father who will deny his own child! By the cruelty of your words, you have denied your son a place amongst the angels in Heaven and have turned me out from my own rath and my own people. Your soul is doubly damned!'

The boy, however, was not to be moved. 'Go!' he shouted. 'You have shamed both me and my family by your baseless accusations. I will hear you no more, nor will I acknowledge your fairy brat as my own son!'

The priest stepped forward. 'You have heard what the Son of Adam has said,' he rebuked the fairy. 'Now be on your way, and trouble my congregation no further!'

Dramatically, he raised his hand and pointed her away from the door of the chapel. The boy and his father turned back into the church.

The fairy's grief was awesome to behold. Overhead, the sky darkened with tempestuous clouds, and a shrill wind began to rise from the direction of the lough. It whipped around the walls of the venerable building, wailing like a banshee, rattling at the windows as though demanding entrance. A finger of lightning flickered in the sky overhead, and thunder boomed far off in the distance with a terrible sound.

The fairy woman lifted the child above her head. It screamed fiercely, but she held it in an iron grip.

'If you will not accept my child freely by baptism into your mortal world,' she cried, 'then take it without my blessing. It shall never be accepted by the lords of the Sídhe, so let it lie among the followers of the White Christ.' And so saying, she threw the child through the door of the church, directly at the font by the priest's hand.

The infant screamed loudly. As it struck the font with a loud crack, it dissolved into a cloud of smoke, which dissipated throughout the church. As all eyes were fixed upon it, no one was looking at the fairy woman; but when they turned to her again, she too had vanished.

The day, however, remained dark and gloomy, with ominous, rolling clouds. And when the font was examined, it was found to have a large crack along one side, as if it had been struck by a heavy weight.

It is said that the church was reconsecrated, because of the contamination by the strange smoke which had blown through it, and that a new baptismal font was put in — the old one was thrown away. Never again did a fairy come to the doors of the church; but, by the same token, neither the boy who had been accused of fathering the child nor his own father ever prospered again. They lost money, and eventually they had to sell their land and move away. That's what comes of being involved too closely with the fairies.

The above story has a number of variations all over Ireland. One variant, which was at one time particularly widespread, comes from Hilltown in County Down, and for many years local people could name the family involved, as they still lived in the district. The cracked baptismal font remained for some time, well outside the precincts of the local church. The County Roscommon variant, however, has an especial resonance, as St Thomas's Abbey near Lough Urlaur was believed to have been possessed by the Devil, who had to be driven out by a drunken piper from County Clare named Donagh O'Grady. It was widely believed in this area that both the Evil One and dark fairies still lingered close by and were ready to tempt mortals at every conceivable opportunity. In some accounts, the church is said to have been a Protestant one, and the name of the young man concerned is given as Robert Ormsby, who was later a rackrenting landlord and priest-hunter in the area. The Ormsbys were believed to have dealt frequently with the fairies, who had many children by them.

These and other accounts also contain a suggestion that fairy women actively sought out male partners from the mortal world in order that any offspring might have a chance of Heaven. All fairies were denied entrance to Paradise (see Chapter Six) due to the fact that they had no souls and had not received Christian baptism. The gates of Heaven, however, stood open to all baptised mortals. Even though the heavenly pleasures were denied to them, many fairy women felt that their offspring might attain Paradise if they had at least some human blood in their veins. By having a human father, the infant could also lay claim – if acknowledged – to a human baptism, which would secure entrance to Paradise at the end of all things.

However, since it was against the laws of the Church to consort with fairies, many human fathers refused to acknowledge their fairy children and rebuffed their former lovers, as in the tale above. The child, neither wholly fairy nor wholly human, could not be accepted by the fairy kind in their raths and mounds and so was turned out to fend for itself in the wider world. It was forced to live alone, well away from the main fairy habitations, and to make its own way as best it could. These abandoned fairy children, it has been argued, formed the basis of the leprechaun belief.

The frequency of alleged unions between humans and fairies, giving rise to large numbers of offspring, may give some credence to the supposition that the leprechaun is a kind of 'halfling', caught somewhere between the two species. Certainly, he has some attributes which might be considered to be the result of human parentage.

Firstly, there is his hair-colour. Many leprechauns are described as being red-haired or having a certain ruddiness about them. Red is not a colour which occurs naturally in the fairy world. Indeed, the colour red is often counted as anathema to both fairies and witches. For example, in many parts of Ireland and Scotland, strands of red thread were woven into the tails of grazing cattle to prevent fairies (or local witches) from stealing their milk, while red ribbon or red thread entwined with straw ('the straw halter') was placed around the neck of a churn during the butter-making process to prevent the fairies from stealing the produce. Celtic people, however, were often red-haired, and the leprechaun's hair-colour is therefore suggestive of a union which is not within the fairy world but rather between fairy and human.

Other leprechauns have occasionally been described as being fair-haired. Again, blond hair is unusual in the fairy world, and this colouring may be representative of the Viking settlers who inhabited parts of Ireland during the ninth, tenth and eleventh centuries. While the majority of these settlers dwelt in largely enclosed city-states — Dublin, Waterford, Wexford, Limerick, Cork, and so on — there is much evidence that they did in fact marry outside the perimeters of such areas, mostly amongst the local Irish and others. This gave rise to a race of people in both Ireland and Scotland who were known as 'Gael-Goidl' (foreign Gaels), and it may be that the leprechaun is somehow related to this particular race, as his hair-colour may denote.

Secondly, there is the question of the leprechaun's general complexion. He is frequently described as ugly or rough-looking, and as having a swarthy skin. This is in contrast to all descriptions of the Tuatha de Danann, who are described as graceful, fine-featured, pale or golden-skinned, and beautiful. It has been suggested that the Tuatha de Danann might have been of Greek origin (as they came from the East) and that they may have had classical Greek features. This, again, is in marked contrast to the leprechaun's general appearance, suggesting that the sprite has his origins in some sub-species of fairy (who perhaps came from somewhere other than Ireland) or in the human world.

Thirdly, there is the matter of the leprechaun's temperament and his general isolation from the majority of the fairy world. While he is certainly not the only fairy who might be regarded as solitary — the banshee, the pouka and the dullahan are also so regarded (although these beings may be more closely allied to the worlds of ghosts and demons than to that of the fairies) — he is undoubtedly the most notable. Some of the possible reasons for his isolation have already been mentioned, but there is little doubt that both his manners and his way of life also serve to alienate him from the rest of the more homogeneous fairy throng. The leprechaun is a loner, and has little time for the frivolities and intrigues of the localised fairy courts.

Life in the fairy mounds is said to be 'gracious and languid' and 'one of great ease'. In each mound, a local fairy king and his queen are supposedly adored by their court, though one gathers that the fairy courts are not all that different from those of the human world. Both contain their spats, jealousies and rivalries between courtiers; both are places of great intrigue, rumour and gossip; and both are places where individual courtiers flit in and out of favour. The fairy court is, in fact, noted for its capricious nature and for its shallowness. It is also noted for its idleness. The leprechaun, of course, has little time for this, for he has a very different disposition from the fairy courtiers.

The trooping fairies regard the leprechaun as dirty, rough, vulgar and uncouth, while he in turn considers them fickle, shallow, feckless, stupid and idle. Contact between the two branches of fairydom is kept to a minimum — although there are occasions, as we shall see later, when communication between them is essential. The fairy throng lives for the praise and approval of others, while the leprechaun needs no such flattery.

These great differences in temperament, style and outlook may indicate a difference in origins. The leprechaun is thought to come from a more pragmatic stock (which may have contained some human elements), while the fairy kind of the mounds and raths may be the direct descendants of the ancient Tuatha de Danann.

This theory does not explain the preponderance of males in the leprechaun line. It may be that some races tend to produce more male offspring than female (just as some human families do), and this may account for the large male leprechaun populace.

However, as has already been intimated, there are female creatures which — while not being counted as leprechauns by the purists — exhibit some of the traits which characterise the leprechaun world. It is to these creatures that we must now turn our attention.

FEMALE LEPRECHAUN-CREATURES

Because many fairies are shape-shifters, having the ability to take on the form of any person or creature they please, the notion of gender in the fairy world has always been slightly problematical. Nevertheless, we can make some form of gender generalisations about some of the leprechaun-like sprites that inhabit this realm.

The grogoch, a North Antrim leprechaun who is often overly helpful to farmers and housewives in that area, has already been discussed. In Antrim, the creature is invariably male; but, as has been noted, this is not the case everywhere. On the Isle of Arran and in the Western Highlands, the being is exclusively female. In her book *The Supernatural Highlands* (1997), Frances Thompson writes:

> [The gruagach] *is a female spectre of the class of brownies to which Highland dairymaids made frequent libations of fresh milk. She frisked and gambolled about the cattle pens and folds, armed only with a pliable reed, with which she switched all who annoyed her by uttering obscene language, or by neglecting to leave for her a share of the dairy produce. In Gaelic,* gruagach *is a word meaning 'wizard-champion' and is, strangely, masculine.*

The main function of the gruagach, she goes on, is to preside over the cattle and to take an interest in matters pertaining to them. A description given by a woman on the island of Heisgeir, off North Uist, who saw the gruagach moving about by the light of the moon, states that she has a full conical hat and a rich mantle of golden hair falling down around her shoulders, and that with a slight swish of her wand she could skilfully admonish some nearby cow. She was habitually seen (and heard) in the grounds of an old nunnery, where her melodious voice sang snatches of an eerie song which was carried about the island on the wind.

The *New Statistical Account for Scotland* (1842), dealing with the parish of Kilmuir in Skye, states:

> *Even so late as 1770, the dairy-maids who attended a herd of cattle on the island of Trodda were in the habit of pouring daily a quantity of milk in a hollow stone for the gruagach. Should they neglect to do so, they were sure of feeling the effects of the brownie the next day. It is said that the Reverend Donald MacQueen, the then minister of the parish, went purposely to Trodda to check that gross superstition. He might have succeeded for a time in doing so, but it is known that many believed in the gruagach's existence long after that reverend gentleman's death.*

Another account of the gruagach or grogoch was given in 1895; it comes from West Brennan, on Arran Island in the Firth of Clyde. This particular creature reputedly lived in a place called Uamh na Gruagaich, or sometimes Uamh na Beiste (the Cave of the Grogoch or Cave of the Monster). This being was certainly female, for she herded, milked and tended the cattle of Brennan, which was a female task there. Indeed, so diligent was she that no spring loss, no death loss, no mishap or disease ever befell the herd, and the cattle were the healthiest and fattest in all the Isles. In the morning, just before first light, the grogoch could be heard tending the animals and singing a melodious air in a clear and beautiful voice. It is said that she would wait on a hillock until the cattle were left for her supervision, but if any human approached her, she would disappear in the twinkling of an eye. If anyone attempted to capture her, it would be the worse for him or her.

The writer and folklorist Otta Swire, in *The Outer Hebrides and Their Legends* (1963), states:

> *In old Gaelic, the word* gruagach *meant 'young chief', or more literally 'long-haired one'. Later it came to be used of a spirit and in some districts (in Skye), a long-haired youth in a fine white shirt (often frilled) and knee-breeches; but more frequently in Skye the Gruagach was a very tall, thin woman with her hair falling to her feet; she wore a soft, misty robe, the effect being described as like a 'white reflection or shade'. She was usually the former mistress of the house or land she haunted, who had either died in childbirth or been put under enchantment. She belonged to the site and not to the occupant and she was seldom seen unless something was about to happen at that site. She helped the owners by caring for cattle and small children (so long as they allowed no dog near her) and the simple were also under her protection. Like the English Brownie, she was partial to a dish of cream. She could sometimes be seen weeping or showing great joy.*

Many of the characteristics of the above grogoch also apply to the gleistig — another female leprechaun-like creature in the Western Highlands. Like the grogoch, she lives in remote and isolated places — caves, old ruins, gullies and abandoned houses — and largely shuns mortals whenever she can. There are few descriptions of her, but she is described as an untidy and dirty creature (like her male equivalent), with green hair and long yellow teeth. However, she is quite harmless and will do a good turn if called upon to do so.

In Ireland, there exists a solitary, female leprechaun-like creature known as the vanathee (from the Irish *bean an tí* — woman of the house). This is a small, diligent woman — very much like the grogoch, but much more tidy and ordered — who will do tasks about the house to help the family to whom she attaches herself. She is, however, rather capricious and fickle in her ways, and will often attach herself to those who do not really deserve her attentions — the lazy and the slovenly — while ignoring those who would clearly benefit from her help. A libation of milk or cream should be left for her by the hearthside, and on no account must any attempt be made to see her as she performs her duties or collects her reward; otherwise, she will abandon the family concerned and will not return. Descriptions of her vary, but she is usually regarded as being extremely small, dressed in a green skirt and white blouse, with a small cap on her head. It has also been suggested that she is rather ugly, and this may link her to the leprechaun.

Like the male grogoch, the vanathee is sometimes more of a hindrance than a help — although it has to be said that such instances are not very frequent. Occasionally, however, she will break or crack plates, move things around so that they can't be found, or accidentally spill things in closed cupboards. In fact, she is often used as an explanation for all the little 'accidents' which happen around the house.

In Ireland, vanathees are widely scattered across the country; in Brittany they are much more common, albeit in a slightly different form. Here, such female sprites attach themselves to houses rather than to families, and will usually aid the particular family that lives in a dwelling, even though this family may change from time to time. If the house is abandoned, the fairy continues to live there in even greater isolation, even if the dwelling should crumble around her.

The most famous of all such solitary female fairies is

La Fée de Lanascol — a leprechaun-like sprite who inhabited the ruined château of Lanascol in rural Lower Brittany and who, at one time, was famous throughout France. Although the château no longer stands, it was at one time a ruin, badly overgrown and falling in on itself. The name of the important local family who owned it has been all but forgotten in the district, but in the past a fairy made the derelict place very much her home, in the style of the Irish leprechaun.

The manor house at Lanascol must at one time have been an extremely important building, boasting extensive grounds crisscrossed by splendid avenues and walkways, and with a grand and sweeping driveway leading up to it. Much of this is now gone, vanished beneath a carpet of leaves and advancing grasses. By the nineteenth century, the house itself had all but disappeared under wild creepers and vines. But the fairy was known to be still there. Many people claimed to have seen her, sweeping leaves and moss from the once grand driveway or working at an overgrown bush in the once well-tended lawns.

Descriptions of her vary, for her clothing appears to differ from season to season, blending with her surroundings — if it is autumn, for example, she wears dull russet hues; if it is spring, she wears vibrant, green-tinged clothing. Sometimes she appears leaning on a crutch, in the form of an old and decrepit hag; sometimes she trips along the weedy walkways in the guise of a young maiden. At other times, she seems to be a grand lady who advances amid the overgrown parkland with an extremely stately bearing (in this guise she is often said to be followed by several small and utterly silent men, all dressed completely in black). As she passes, the ancient copper beeches which still line the driveway bow down as if to a queen, and the water will tremble at her gaze.

The villagers — many of whom are farmers and labourers — all fear meeting with her, for she can be regarded as a bad omen. If seen, she must not be approached, they warn. They refer to her as the 'groac'h Lanascol', or sometimes simply as 'the lady'.

In former times, she was said to be the guardian of a fabulous treasure, hidden somewhere in the vicinity of the fallen château many years ago. This, of course, gives her the same status as the Irish leprechaun, who is also said to guard immeasurable wealth from former times. Indeed, it is said that the Fée was so wealthy that, when the Lanascol estate was put up for public auction by the Public Notary at Plouaret, it was the fairy herself who bought the château and its grounds, and she is said to have remained their owner ever since.

This fairy is not unique in Breton folklore; there are many tales from all over Brittany of solitary female fairies living in ruined châteaux or manor houses. Professor Anatole le Braz, author of such works as La Legende de la Mort and Au Pays des Pardons, states that 'Brittany has always been a kingdom of Fairie. One cannot even travel a league without brushing past the habitation of some male or female fairy.' Many of these dwellings resemble the leprechaun's, and many Breton fées can be seen almost as 'female leprechauns'.

While not even the fairy of Lanascol, eerie though she is, is regarded as wholly evil, the same cannot be said for her sisters in Kintail in Scotland. Here, there is also a tradition of female fairies living alone in inaccessible places; but these are to be avoided at all costs. They are eaters of human flesh and drinkers of human blood. Although they resemble the traditional leprechaun in that they are (in their original form) naturally ugly and unkempt, they are also dangerous shape-shifters and can therefore take on any form. However, they have cloven feet like a goat's, a telltale sign which they

cannot disguise. Their prey is the shepherds and cow-
herds who come to the remote places where they dwell
in order to keep watch over their flocks or herds.

A story from Kintail records how the fairy uses her
evil wiles against mortals.

*Three men were hunting among the hills of Kintail.
They had hunted all day, and as night came on, they
took shelter in an old shieling [hut] that was used by
the shepherds of that area. They lit a fire, cooked
some meat that they'd caught, and generally made
themselves comfortable on some dry grass and
moss. Two of them sat on one side of the fire while
the third, on the other side, played a trump [a jew's
harp].*

*One of the pair began to talk of the day's hunting,
of how long they'd been away from home and how
he wished that he had his sweetheart with him. The
other one expressed a similar sentiment. Now this
was a foolish thing to do, since it is widely believed
in Kintail that it is imprudent to wish for anything
at night without first invoking the protection of the
Deity, and this neither man had done.*

*Almost at once, the door of the shieling opened
and a woman entered. The fire had well burned
down by now and threw out only a faint light, so
none of the men could see very well, but each of the
pair was sure that it was his sweetheart come to see
him. Each thought he saw a different woman, you
see. She sat down between them and put her arms
affectionately around them, cuddling up to each one
in turn.*

*The musician sat on the other side of the dim fire,
watching this going on. Then, to his horror, he saw a
thin stream of blood trickling towards him across the
hearthstones. At the same time, he was able to see*

that the woman had the feet of a deer or a goat, and he knew immediately that this was a solitary fairy who lived in the high hills of Kintail and attacked travellers and wayfarers through her domain. The others could not see the danger — all each man saw was his own sweetheart.

In terror, the musician started up and dashed out of the hut. The fairy, realising that she had been discovered, leapt up after him and pursued him from the place, galloping after him like the wind. He ran as fast as he could, and it was only thanks to his considerable physical fitness that he was able to out-distance her.

At last he reached the doorway of the nearest human habitation, and at this the fairy ceased her pursuit. He was brought in, white and trembling, and had to be revived by good mountain spirits before he could even tell what had happened.

The next morning the musician, together with some other men and a priest, went back to the shieling in the hills, where they found the badly mangled bodies of his two companions. Both of them had been drained of all their blood. Of the evil lone fairy, there was no sign; but every man there (including the priest) had the distinct impression that she was somewhere close by, maybe even watching them. That's the way of it with her kind.

Such blood-drinking female leprechaun-like creatures were also reported in some old folk-tales from Kerry (particularly in the Magillicuddy Reeks and in the parish of Sneem). These were foul sprites who chiefly attacked those who refused to abide by the Black Fast during Lent (when even milk products were forbidden by the Church, and so tea was 'black') or who were morally lax in other ways. Sean O'Sullivan (himself a Kerryman), the famous archivist of the Folklore Commission during the 1950s and early 60s, claimed to know of a fortress in the Reeks where these creatures resided. He mentioned this during a lecture in 1961, but it was never followed up, and the location of the place appears to have been lost. Perhaps this is just as well!

Although there appear to be no female leprechauns in the strictest sense of the term, then, there are a number of feminine sprites and fairies who, by virtue of their rather solitary condition and of their functions, seem to be related — albeit sometimes obliquely — to the leprechaun world. If there are any females of the pure leprechaun classification, they keep themselves extremely well hidden!

Age

Although no reliable way to test the age of a leprechaun has yet been found, there is no doubt that each individual is incredibly old. It is said that the youngest of them can vividly remember 'the days of Noll Cromwell in Ireland' (the 1650s), while the oldest of them state that they were here when the first Celts arrived (about 250 BC). Some folklorists have attributed this to so much blarney on the part of the leprechauns, but there may be at least some truth in these claims.

In order to find out anything about the age of a leprechaun, it is necessary to trick him into revealing it. This is not as easy as it may sound, for leprechauns, being expert tricksters themselves, are not easily fooled. It is not enough to say, for example, 'I'm sure that you remember such-and-such [some great event long past]'; the leprechaun will sense what you are about and feed you inaccurate information concerning the event. This will, in the end, cause you to doubt whether the leprechaun was there or not.

A favourite trick of those desirous to know the true age of a leprechaun is, therefore, to reverse the process and give the leprechaun inaccurate information. Many leprechauns are full of their own importance as far as historical matters are concerned, and regard humans as rather stupid beings with no knowledge of history whatsoever. Therefore, one might, for instance, engage the leprechaun in conversation thus: 'Ah, that Noll Cromwell — wasn't he a great and fine man? Didn't he serve the Irish people well? I hear that they're erecting a monument to him in O'Connell Street in Dublin for all his kindness and charitable works here.'

At this, the leprechaun will become terribly indignant, because none of his tribe have a shred of regard for Oliver Cromwell. (There is an old legend that the Lord Protector of England lured several of them onto an open Bible, which he then slammed shut, trapping them inside the Holy Word forever. In parts of County Clare, this act of base treachery is ascribed to Edmund Ludlow, the Cromwellian officer who led the first troops into the Burren. However, the tale of 'Cromwell's Bible' still remains a sore point with many leprechauns, and his name must be spoken judiciously in their presence.) In reply to this insult, the leprechaun will answer: 'Sure, wasn't he the most black-hearted cur that ever set foot in Ireland? Sure, I well mind myself....'

And, in his rage, he will launch into a personal anecdote about Cromwellian times in Ireland, in order to prove his point. By doing so, he is proving that he was alive during the period, and this may be used to gauge his approximate age. Of course, such calculations may be wildly inaccurate.

By contrast, most Irish leprechauns practically idolise Brian Boru — the great High King of Ireland during the late tenth and early eleventh centuries — and every

leprechaun will swear that he was at the Battle of
Clontarf in 1014, when, according to their tradition,
'great Brian drove the heathen Dane from the shores of
Ireland'. Most of these stories are greatly exaggerated,
although there may be some evidence that leprechauns
were around at the time. However, it is extremely
unlikely that any of them were involved in the fighting
or that any of them sat, as their tradition states, 'on
Brian's shoulder so that they could offer him advice'.

Several leprechauns claim connections with other
ancient kings. In fact, some claim association with the
very Viking kings whom Brian and his forces drove out
of Ireland. According to some traditions in Meath, for
instance, at the Beltane Fair of 1898, a leprechaun by
the name of Michael O'Reirdon, from County Wicklow,
stated that he had been the chief advisor to King
Ivarr II, Norse king of Dublin, prior to his defeat by the
Dalriadic clans of Argyll in 914 AD. O'Reirdon then
went on to allege that it was because Ivarr paid no heed
to the advice which the leprechaun had given him that
he was defeated in Scotland. (It should be remembered,
however, that before making his assertions, Michael
O'Reirdon had consumed a vast quantity of poteen.)
Several other leprechauns have claimed more tenuous
links with Viking kings in both Limerick and Cork. It
is through these connections that leprechauns have
learned the locations of Viking treasure-hoards, which
has propelled them to their position as the bankers of
the fairy world (see Chapter Four).

Some leprechauns claim to be even older, stating
that they can remember Irish kings before the time of
recorded history. Many claim to have known Niall of
the Nine Hostages — one of the great High Kings of
Ireland, who led a number of successful expeditions
into other parts of the ancient world — although their
descriptions of the man and his temperament vary

greatly. Some describe him as a great and powerful warrior of a 'kindly disposition', while others claim that he was 'a smallish man with a bad and surly temper on him'. Incidentally, conflicting accounts and descriptions of Brian Boru (whom many leprechauns claim to have known personally) are also given. He is described as a 'young and fearless warrior, galloping into battle at the head of his troops against the Danish foe'. At the time of Clontarf, Brian was seventy-two, and although he was killed by a Manx warrior, he took no real part in the fighting.

Through their association with these ancient Irish kings, leprechauns also have access to the buried gold and jewels, hidden during wars and plagues, which are left over from those times. In fact, it is said that the laughremen of South Armagh guard a fabulous treasure which is supposed to lie near Emhain Macha (Navan Fort), the seat of the ancient kings of Ulster and some High Kings of Ireland.

Across the Celtic world, some leprechaun-creatures claim an even greater longevity. The town of Newlyn in Cornwall boasts a solitary being known as 'the Tolcarne Troll' (although the use of the description 'troll' may be inaccurate). He is described as 'a little pleasant-looking old man' in a tight leather jerkin, with a great hood or cowl over his head. He is generally untidy and easy-going in his ways (and in this, he roughly corresponds to the representation of the leprechaun). Generally invisible, he makes his presence known by tiny sounds and grunts at the place where he dwells (an odd outcropping of greenstone known as Newlyn Tolcarne, which was used by the druids for their rites in times long past).

This little gentleman claims that he was alive in early biblical times, and that he originally came from what is now the Holy Land. In fact, he states that he came to

Cornwall on a Phoenician ship trading for tin. He had
spent his early years on various vessels sailing between
Tyre (which was a large Phoenician city at the time)
and the coasts of Cornwall and Ireland. After falling out
with one of the captains, he was abandoned on the
coast near Newlyn, where he remained, waiting for a
Phoenician boat to return and take him home. None
came, and he was forced to remain where he was.

Many stories have grown up around him — the
chief one being that he acted as an oracle to Hiram,
King of Tyre (in the Lebanon), and that he assisted in
the building of Solomon's holy temple in Israel. (Hiram
and Solomon were contemporaries, and, according to
the Bible, Hiram did in fact supply cedars from his
estates in Lebanon for the construction of Solomon's
temple.) In some variations of his story, however, he is
described as 'Odin the Wanderer' or simply as 'the
Wanderer', which connects him with the religion and
folklore of the Vikings. He was also supposed to guard
an enchanted glass known as the Mirror of the Ages,
which could show past, present and future. Anyone
could look into this mirror, provided he gave the little
creature a tot of dark rum. Through the glass, people
could behold what their ancestors had done in previous
times, although they might not like what they saw.

As to the Troll's age, it was said that he was old even
when the Pyramids were raised. Other fairies in
Cornwall claim to remember the destruction of Sodom
and Gomorrah, and some can even recall Noah's flood.
In Cornwall, such assertions may well be taken as the
truth; but in Ireland, where the leprechauns are full of
blether, blarney and poteen, they should be treated
with grave suspicion.

Because of the exaggerations and outright lies of the
Irish fairies, the true age of a leprechaun is very difficult
to ascertain. As with all questions to a leprechaun, the

investigator will probably never receive a satisfactory answer and will be forced to rely on guesswork. Leprechauns like to cultivate an air of mystery — and what better subjects for this than their origins and their age? All that we can say with certainty is that they are all probably very old.

However, the record for longevity probably belongs to an aged-looking grogoch in North Antrim. When asked what age he might be, he replied, 'I have existed since the foundation of the world.' Now that's old!

Chapter Four

Leprechaun Professions

Traditionally, the most common profession for the leprechaun is that of fairy shoemaker. He is said to prepare and mend shoes for the Macara Shee (the trooping fairies) so that they can go out on their travels through the countryside and attend grand balls and céilís within the fairy mounds and raths. Some accounts portray him as a shoemaker, actually preparing new shoes for the fairy balls, while others state that he is a shoe-repairer or cobbler, simply restoring those shoes which have been worn out by the unending dancing and frivolity.

Perhaps this distinction comes from a time when shoes and boots were expensive and much-prized items of clothing. About a century ago, many rural people still generally went about in bare feet and only wore shoes sporadically — if they owned a pair at all! Old local tales contain accounts of country children going to school in towns like Limerick and Waterford with their shoes hung around their necks, only putting them on when they reached the town limits. In Coleraine, in North Derry, there is a spot formerly known as the Barefoot Burn, where the country children washed their feet before putting on their boots to enter the town. Even as recently as the middle of the last century, most people in Ireland owned only one pair of boots, which lasted them the greater part of their lives. Itinerant shoe-menders who travelled from one place to another, then, were welcomed into communities and were counted as extremely important people, since they were the only ones with sufficient know-how to repair shoes and boots.

The leprechaun, by association with these artisans, became a central figure in the fairy world. Fairies loved dancing and were always engaged in some ball or céilí, which often left their shoes in need of serious repair. Perhaps this was the origin of the word 'leprechaun', which, as we have already noted, may come from the ancient Irish *leith bhrógán* (half-shoe-maker): he repaired one shoe, half of a pair — the most worn shoe which the fairy had ruined with its dancing.

In many tales concerning leprechauns, the creature gives away his position in drains and ditches by the tapping of his tiny hammer as he worked on a shoe or boot. He is to be seen with his last and waxed strings, sitting cross-legged (in the fashion of country tailors and shoe-menders) in the shade of a bush or the stump of a tree, or in the dry part of some gully. If he is so absorbed, then it is worthwhile to make a sudden grab for him, to see if he can be caught.

However, shoemaking is not the only form of employ-ment in which the leprechaun can be engaged. There are numerous stories which speak of leprechauns under-taking other forms of work, for the sprite is nothing if not highly industrious and enterprising in his choice of occupations.

Leprechauns as Builders

It is thought that the earliest forms of leprechauns or leprechaun-like fairies were not shoe-menders at all, but rather builders and stonemasons. This theory probably has its origins in the number of tiny piles or hummocks of stones to be found in fields and moors throughout the Celtic countryside. In Ireland, these were known as 'leachts' and were said to mark the spots where victims had died during the Great Famine of 1845–52. There may, however, be an older explanation, for these stone piles clearly existed long before the nineteenth century. It is said that they once marked the sites of leprechauns' houses, and that they were erected by the wee folk as signals that no one else could build there.

In some areas of the Celtic world, leprechaun-like people were credited with building the mounds and tumuli in which the Tuatha de Danann came to dwell. They may also have been associated with tiny settlements of stone houses to be found in the Orkneys (Skara Brae) and on the northern islands of Sanday and Westray, since these buildings are very small. Old stories around such places speak of tiny groups of builders – a small, wizened people from the north – who built their communities in extremely isolated and inhospitable places, mainly on islands. The bulk of these houses were underground, to protect them from the fierce winds and sand which blew across these places in the winter months. The tiny people were said to be skilled at building and stonemasonry, but they kept themselves (and their secrets) to themselves, preferring to stay well away from other islanders. They were farmers, keeping cattle and carving out small cultivated areas for themselves, but they were also sometimes counted as supernatural beings with strange and magical ways. They seem to have vanished just as mysteriously as they came, leaving only their houses behind them. Because they lived mostly underground, later peoples saw them as fairies, brownies or leprechaun-like beings.

The notion that leprechauns might live underground was once widespread in several parts of Ireland — for example, Cork, Limerick, Clare and Westmeath. On the islands off the Irish coast, too, they built underground shelters for themselves and for other fairies.

For mortal people, living side by side with such builders was not always easy. An old tale from Rathlin Island in North Antrim speaks of fairies who decided to build a new house close to a human settlement:

There was a man on Rathlin called Tommy Anderson, one time, and he had the notion of building a new house. It was not for himself, you understand, but for his mother, who'd become very old and infirm. Her name was Peggy Bradley and she was a widow woman and couldn't get about all that much. He thought that they could all live together in the one house, and that he and his wife could look after her. He built a place up at Cabbal, near the West Lighthouse — a right tidy place it was — and lived there snug enough for a while.

One evening they were all teeming potatoes by the door, and the water was running everywhere. There was a sharp and angry knock on the door, and when Tommy went to see what it was, there was a wee runt of a man in a skirty coat waiting for him. He was an ugly wee fellow, all burned with the sun and wearing a pair of oul' brogues on him that no tinker would wear. And he had a pipe rammed in the corner of his mouth like a sailor.

Tommy knew that this was one of the Thane-a-korr [the local name for a leprechaun-like creature], *and he asked him what he wanted.*

The little man said that he had been building houses for the fairy people in that particular area, and that the potato water was causing everybody great distress. He also told Tommy that this place was now a fairy place, and that he and his family would have to move on and let the little man build more fairy houses (which were underground, if you understand). If he didn't, the Thane-a-korr would take their vengeance and would make life very miserable for himself and his old mother. In the meantime, he was to stop teeming potatoes by the cottage doorway.

And with that, the little man turned and was gone without a by-your-leave.

Tommy took it all very seriously, for he didn't want to get on the wrong side of the fairy builders, and so he moved all his family to another part of the island, and the grand, tidy house that he'd built was eventually pulled down.

There's people that will tell you that there's still fairy building going on up at Cabbal yet. It's a fairy place, all right. Not even the lighthouse-men would go near it.

It appears that the leprechaun-builders put what amounted to a compulsory purchase order on Tommy Anderson's new house, and that, like many other developers, they showed scant regard towards those who were already living there.

Leprechauns often built underground fairy dwellings wherever they wished, and this could be difficult for humans living in the vicinity. Some of the most favoured constructions were 'céilí-houses' — places where fairies would gather to make merry. This could often lead to excessive noise and clamour, particularly at night when humans were trying to sleep. There was really nothing that they could do; like Tommy Anderson in the above story, they would have to move elsewhere. The best they could hope for was that no leprechauns would choose to build dwellings within their immediate vicinity.

Leprechauns as Metalworkers and Smiths

In some respects, leprechauns share certain work-related characteristics with the goblins of Germany and Switzerland. These little fellows are often described as both miners and metalworkers and are skilled in forging iron and copper. In parts of Ireland and Scotland, too, leprechauns and brownies are sometimes described as tinkers and metal-beaters rather than as shoe-menders or cobblers. The tapping which humans sometimes hear is not always the sound of the sprite working on a brogue or a shoe; sometimes it is the noise of him repairing an old pot or pan or shaping a bit of pliable metal.

Although some leprechauns are particularly skilled in metalwork — examples of their work are often seen at the fairy fairs and goblin markets which are to be found in remote areas of the Celtic countries — the majority of them are not. They can temporarily patch up broken implements, but this is really the extent of their expertise. This lack of specialised skill, however, does not prevent them from setting up as skilled tinsmiths, even though the work that they produce is quite often sub-standard and shoddy. Nor does it prevent them from claiming great skills — many will assert, for example, that they have been metalworkers and even goldsmiths to the great High Kings of Ulster, especially Brian Boru (again) and Niall of the Nine Hostages.

Leprechauns — particularly the larger varieties — sometimes also claim some skill as blacksmiths. In many rural areas, blacksmiths also served as metalworkers, making kettles, pots and pans for the people, and this fits in well with the leprechaun's exaggerated claims of skill in that area.

It is quite probable that most of these sprites have been nowhere near an ordinary horse, because most animals show a particular aversion to the fairy kind; nevertheless, the leprechaun may declare himself to be a master blacksmith who will only work with 'horses of the fairy kind'. It has to be said straight away that these are not horses as we mortals understand them. Rather, they are the appearance of horses — old sticks, brooms or hurdles that have been transformed into the likeness of horses through fairy glamour. By pretending to shoe these creatures, the leprechaun perpetuates the illusion and so deceives those who are watching him.

It must be pointed out that the leprechaun will not operate his own forge, as a blacksmith might in the human world. Rather, he will take over an old forge which has been abandoned or allowed to fall into ruin and neglect, and use it for his own purposes. It is said that the ghosts of the dead often congregate at such places, and leprechauns appear to have the power to commandeer these spirits into helping them in their 'work'. The ghosts of the unshriven dead — particularly those who had died suddenly, perhaps in some accident — were especially vulnerable to leprechaun influence (see 'Leprechauns and the Dead', Chapter Six).

The following story reflects the power which the leprechauns sometimes had over the souls of the dead. Elements of the descriptions of the fairies reflect the dwarfish German metalworkers. The story itself comes from Galway.

Near the old church at Kilmacduagh, there is a long bridge over a river. Just beyond the end of this bridge there used to be an old forge standing. It used to belong to two brothers named Gregory, who were famous in the locality as blacksmiths. However, they were both great drunkards, and in the end they had to give up the smithying completely on account of bad health.

The old forge went to wrack and ruin, and never a one went near it, for it was said far and near that the place was badly haunted. When houses, churches or blacksmiths' forges are left to their ruin, they draw ghosts and phantoms to them — that's a well-known fact. They said that on certain nights of the year — the old festival seasons — there were lights about it, coming and going, like men carrying lamps and lanterns. It was said, too, that you could hear men talking and arguing even though there was no-body there. There were those who would have told you that the place was fairy-haunted, and that little men in bottle-green coats and old-fashioned three-cornered hats and knee-britches could be seen there at all hours of the day.

But it was at night that it was at its most ghostly. There's many that said they could hear the sound of a hammer striking on iron as soon as the sun started to go down, as though men were making horseshoes there. Nobody would go near it, even between the lights [at twilight], *for fear of what they might see, for there were queer, broken shadows all about the old place.*

There was a man called Anthony Hynds that lived over beyond the bridge, and when he had drink on him, he was afraid of nothing and would do anything for a dare. One evening in the pub, when he had a right drop about him, some of his neighbours wagered him that he wouldn't go up to the old forge and take a look in.

Now it was near to Hallowe'en, which is always a bad time of the year for ghosts and fairies. It is said that around this time, the leprechauns have the power to take you away with them into the Beyond, and it is well to stay close to your fire and not go venturing about places that are known to be haunted. But Anthony Hynds had the drink-courage on him and would chance anything, so he readily agreed to the wager.

That night, when it was dark and the moon was covered with clouds, he made his way up to the old forge, with his neighbours following a good way behind him to make sure that he carried out the wager. It was a lonely place, sure enough, with the wind soughing in the branches of the old trees that grew around it, like the cry of a banshee. And there were lights coming and going about the smithy, as though somebody was moving about there by the glow of lanterns.

The drink-courage left Anthony Hynds and the sweat stood on his brow like drops of rain, but he'd made a wager with his neighbours and he had to go through with it. He walked along a little laneway that led down to the forge, and stopped in the shade of a great tree to see what was going on. And he could barely believe his eyes.

There around the forge were gathered a number of little men — ugly-looking, they were, with long, long coats on them and old soft hats such as people wore long ago. And the forge was lit, and Anthony could see their faces in its red light — cruel-looking, they all were, to a man. He knew then that they were either fairies or leprechauns and that they were shoeing their horses for a night's mischief.

But there was more, for there were two men

working at the forge, hammering the metal by the light of the forge-flames and the glow of a rush-light. Anthony Hynds said ever after that he knew both the men that worked there, and he said that both of them had died within the year that had just gone. One, he was certain, was Richard Gregory, who used to own the forge and who had died in drink; the other was a man named Lehane, who had died when he was thrown from a grey horse beside the old church at Kilmacduagh. There's always something odd about a grey horse or a red-headed woman, for they say that the leprechauns and the fairy kind always have power over them that meddle with either of those. And those that die in drink leave their souls open to the abuses of the fairy people. That was the way of it, as Anthony Hynds well knew. He saw that if the two men — or ghosts, as they were — did not work fast enough, one of the rough little men would hit them with a switch that he'd cut from a hedge, to make them work faster.

Anthony let a great yell out of him at this terrible sight and turned on his heels and ran back along the laneway, the drink-courage completely deserting him. He never stopped until he had reached the road and was safe among the neighbours that had followed him. Only then did he look back; and when he did so, he saw that the whole place was totally in darkness.

And yet there was many a one that would tell you that when they passed by the old forge, even long afterwards, they could still see strange lights coming and going and they could still hear the sound of hammers striking on metal, as the leprechauns made the souls of them that were recently dead shoe their fairy horses. That was always the way of it, and it's one of the things which the Church won't tell you about.

The above story portrays the leprechauns as smiths and reveals them to be extremely bad-tempered and cruel, much like the German kobolds. While they are certainly not miners in the kobold tradition, the leprechauns display some of the characteristics of these evil dwarves — they employ ghosts to do their work for them, and they treat them abominably. In many tales, these fallen spirits are condemned to serve the leprechauns until the Day of Judgement, as a punishment for their wayward lifestyles when alive.

Leprechauns as Distillers

Reference has already been made to the leprechaun's great skill at (and love of) distilling spirits. In many ways, this reflects the traditions of the Irish peasantry many years ago. Nowadays, we tend to obtain our liquor from public houses or other licensed premises, but in days gone by this was not always the case. Distilling was once quite common in many parts of the country, and many cottages had their own stills. Most country people were able to distil at least some form of spirit — although whether it was actually drinkable or not is open to question! There were those, of course, who were very skilled in the distilling art and could produce spirits of superior quality.

The leprechaun was the most skilled distiller in the fairy world. The poteen which he produced was the sweetest liquor ever tasted. However, few people seem to have tasted it, since the leprechaun appears to consume most of his own produce. Perhaps this is just as well; mortals should never accept drink from a leprechaun, as it will rob them of their senses and take away their memories.

Leprechauns were supposed to provide all the spirits,

wines and ales which were consumed at fairy functions. These were prepared in such a way that, if the fairies were to invite mortals to join in their revelries, those who drank from the 'fairy cup' would forget their homes, their wives and sweethearts, their children and their property, and live amongst the fairies ever after, oblivious to the outside world. It was said that leprechaun poteen was like a drug to the senses of any mortal man or woman.

If fairies were to drink from the cup, however, they would become all the more merry and raucous and would get up to all sorts of mischief and foolery. They would dance longer and much more livelily, they would roar and laugh and tell old stories and sing old songs. The leprechaun's liquor had the effect of making even the gloomiest fairies exceedingly jolly. Sometimes it also made them susceptible to the leprechaun's will, so each proffered draught had to be judged exceedingly carefully.

Leprechauns as Musicians

The leprechaun's abilities as a professional musician have also already been discussed. The leprechaun is a highly skilled musician who has a long memory and remembers old tunes which all mortals (and most fairies) have long forgotten. Indeed, the leprechaun's repertoire stretches back almost to the birth of Celtic music. It is said that the first leprechauns were great harpists, and that they taught the early bards of Ireland their skills and music. Nowadays they are more at home with the fiddle or the Irish pipes, although a number of them are also known to be great bodhrán players.

Most of the tunes they play are so old that they have no titles, and those mortal musicians who sometimes 'borrow' them have to give them names — 'The Hare in the Barley', 'Seamus McInanders' (both relatively well-known tunes, recorded from County Down leprechauns), and so on. Sometimes the stolen leprechaun music is simply given a general title, such as 'The Music of the Ghosts' — a series of consecutive tunes heard and recaptured by a fisherman on Great Blasket, off the Kerry coast. Not that it is easy to steal a leprechaun's tune, for they take their music very seriously and guard their melodies with a fierce jealousy. Any mortal who does manage to steal a melody will usually find that some serious ill befalls him before too long, as the leprechaun takes his revenge.

Leprechauns will usually play only at gatherings, and this is where most of their ancient tunes are to be heard. In order to hear a leprechaun play, one must go to a place where fairies are known to congregate — an old fort or rath, maybe, or simply a riverbank — late in the evening. This is when the 'Good Folk' gather for a céilí, and one is bound to hear at least two or three old tunes. It is, however, advisable to be extremely careful; leprechaun music is known to have an intoxicating effect upon even the dourest mortals, making them leap and dance straight away. There is a famous story, recounted in areas ranging from North Antrim to Limerick, of a woman who overheard the leprechauns playing and danced so enthusiastically that she danced all her toes off!

Interspersed with the music are old stories and ballads sung in the *sean-nós* style (unaccompanied). Despite their rather ugly looks and bedraggled appearance, leprechauns have exceptionally fine singing voices. Indeed, it is said that many great opera stars would give anything to have the pitch and range of a leprechaun in full voice. 'To hear one of them sing,' observed an old Leitrim woman, 'would make the tears start in your eyes.'

Leprechauns are also well-versed in old stories, particularly in ghostly and/or humorous tales. Their memories are phenomenal, and their knowledge of antique Irish texts is unsurpassed. And it is well-known that, their ungainly attributes aside, they are exceptionally fine dancers and can perform jigs and reels to perfection.

In spite of his surly looks, then, the leprechaun can be quite a cultivated fairy when he chooses to be — perhaps even more so than the rather fickle sprites who comprise the Macara Shee. It is little wonder, then, that he is very frequently sought as an entertainer at the fairy balls. However, his price for such services, like any other superstar's, is said to be very high. And it is to leprechauns and money that we must now turn.

LEPRECHAUNS AS BANKERS

There is no doubt that leprechauns are the nearest thing the fairy world has to bank managers. In fact, some folklorists argue that this is their primary function, superseding all of their other occupations.

Leprechauns, it is said, have access to untold wealth. As has already been mentioned, they remember where all the ancient treasures are hidden, all across Ireland. These treasures include the wealth of long-dead Irish kings, the plunder of the Vikings who once raided the coasts, Norman gold and the pillaged booty of pirates. They also know, through supernatural means, where misers have hidden their hoards and local aristocrats have concealed their money against robbery. These hoards add up to a total of millions of pounds, and their exact locations are locked away in each leprechaun's head.

However, the leprechaun is something of a miser

himself and refuses to share this knowledge with any other fairy. Thus, each leprechaun is the guardian of all the secret wealth in Ireland (and perhaps even in other Celtic countries). So when the trooping fairies seek to dispense largesse, or to reward some mortal for some kindness he or she has performed towards them, it is to the leprechaun they must go for money. If, as is sometimes said, a bank manager has a heart of stone, then the heart of the leprechaun is even harder. Seldom does he part with any of the wealth, and he sits as self-appointed judge over the fickle (as he considers it) conduct of the other fairies.

Nor does he keep all this treasure anywhere near his home; it is sufficient for him to know its various locations. However, he will sometimes keep a fraction of it to hand in order to cover any unexpected expenses which he may incur. The gold (for such it is) is usually kept in an old butter-crock, iron pot or some similar container. This has led to the idea — commonly held amongst mortals — that each leprechaun possesses a crock of gold. It is also generally believed that he marks its location with a rainbow — so the crock lies at the end of a natural (or supernatural) phenomenon. All the treasure-hunter has to do, therefore, is follow the rainbow to its end (the place where it appears to touch the ground) in order to find the leprechaun's wealth. As with everything else about the leprechaun tribe, this is not as easy as it first appears; nobody has yet reached the rainbow's end to claim his or her fortune. Many people have spent fruitless days in chasing rainbows, eventually coming away with nothing at all.

In his role as fairy banker, each leprechaun carries with him two black leather pouches. In one there is a silver shilling — which magically returns to the purse every time it is paid out, so that the leprechaun can appear to pay out large sums of money without ever parting with a shilling. In the other pouch he carries a coin of gold — usually from an antique period — with which he will try to bribe his way out of tricky situations. However, those who accept this coin should beware: it will usually turn to leaves or ashes (its natural form) soon after the leprechaun has parted with it. Both these coins serve to confirm the fairy's tricky nature with regard to money.

Tales concerning mortals who try to extract the treasure's whereabouts from a leprechaun are legion throughout Ireland. Leprechauns are naturally suspicious of humans, whom they believe to be rather stupid, inferior creatures, and so they delight in outwitting mortals who try to force them to reveal their hidden riches. If one should catch a leprechaun and demand to be taken to his nearest cache of wealth, one must never take one's eyes off him for a second, or he will disappear in a flash. Hold tight to him and keep concentrating on him until you reach the treasure. Even then, he will try many tricks to escape or to make the riches vanish.

A well-known story, told all over Ireland, illustrates the above point. This particular version of it is from Kerry.

There was a man living near Listowel one time who had a blind sister and an old mother to look after. You can imagine that they were all very poor, and the man had sometimes hardly a rag of a shirt to put on his back.

One day, he was out cutting peats in the bog for the winter stacks. He was just cutting close to what looked like an old bush when he saw a sudden movement under the leaves. He stopped; the leaves rustled again, and out from underneath them came a little man, only a bit longer than a forefinger. He was an untidy-looking creature with a large, wide-brimmed hat and an old claw-hammer coat, black with dirt, across his back. Seeing the man cutting peats, he made a dart to the side and went to disappear into the heather that was growing on the surface of the bog.

But the man was quicker. Almost instinctively, he stuck out his foot and caught the end of the coat as the little man made to dart away. He knew right well that this was a leprechaun and that he had a crock of gold hidden somewhere nearby. If he could get his hands on those riches, his sister and his mother would never have to worry about anything again. And he would be one of the richest men in the county himself.

Bending down, he scooped the little man into the hollow of his hand before he could vanish into the thicket.

'Oh, murther!' screamed the leprechaun. 'It's a bad day in Ireland, to be sure, when an honest tradesman can't go about his business without being set upon by rogues! Not since the days of Black Cromwell — bad cess to his name — was ever a poor and innocent traveller so harried!'

But the man just laughed. 'There's nothing innocent about you, my little maneen,' he exclaimed. 'Now take me to your crock of gold!'

The leprechaun simply made a sound that was somewhere between a snort and a laugh, and spat onto the other's clenched fist. 'Ah, I have no crock of gold!' he replied. 'Sure, and I'm only a poor trades-man — where would I get all the money ye think that I might have? Now put me down, like a sensible fellow, and let me go about my own business!'

But the mortal shook his head. 'Not until ye show me where yer crock of gold lies,' he retorted.

The leprechaun heaved a great sigh. 'That's just an oul' story put about by mortals that know no better!' he insisted. 'I thought that a decent fellow like yourself would have had more wit about you than to believe them. It's well-known that leprechauns such as myself are as poor as church mice, and I'll go bail that you've more money about you at this second than I've had in my whole long life, and that's a fact.'

But the man was not to be turned. He tightened his fist, squeezing the leprechaun mercilessly. 'Where is your crock of gold?' he repeated. 'For I'm not setting you down till you tell me.'

The leprechaun gasped and spluttered. 'All right! All right! Stop yer squeezin'. It's true that I might have a little bit of money put by, but it's hardly worth botherin' about, and it would certainly be of no interest to a fine, well-heeled gentleman such as yerself.'

But his captor was in no mood for his silver-tongued flattery. 'I'll be the judge of that,' he told the leprechaun. 'Take me to it. Is it far from here?'

The leprechaun shook his head. 'Not far,' he said. 'But a decent fellow like yerself wouldn't take away the last penny of an honest artisan, now would he?'

Without a word, the man tightened his grip.

'All right! I'll take you to it.' And, hoisting himself up in the fellow's fist, he pointed out the road that they were to go.

Following the pointing finger, his captor walked all the way down a boreen and over a stile (never once lifting his eyes off the sprite, in case he should disappear) and across several fields. At last they came to a large stand of trees — too big to be called a copse and too small to be called a wood.

'Here we are,' said the leprechaun, pointing into its dark depths. 'I've hidden my poor savings at the

base of one of these trees. Now let me go and be
about my own business.'

But the other kept a tight grip on him. 'Show me
exactly where it is,' he insisted, stepping in amongst
the trees. The fairy had no other option but to remain
where he was and guide his captor into the depths of
the grove.

At length they stopped before a large tree which
didn't look any different from any of the others
around it. The leprechaun waved a hand in its
general direction.

'There it is!' he almost shouted. 'There's where
my poor savings are hidden. And much good may
they do ye. Now let me go, ye bullyin' robber!'

But the man shook his head. 'How do I know that
you're not playin' me for a fool?' he asked. 'You
could point to any oul' tree and tell me that there
was wealth buried under it, and you'd be away, quick
as a wink, before I'd find out yer lies.'

The leprechaun waved a dismissive hand in the
air. 'Very well,' he said in exasperation. 'Was ever
there so much distrust in the heart of a scoundrel
since the days of Black Cromwell? Look at the foot
of the tree, an' I'll show ye the fortune that is lying
there.'

The man looked, but all the same he kept one eye
on the leprechaun in case he would disappear. And
as he looked, he suddenly seemed to see through
the ground, as if he was looking down into a pool of
water; and in a hollow in the roots of the tree he
saw several butter-crocks with gold coins spilling out
of them, and strings of pearls and diamonds lying
beside them. It was a great fortune, to be sure — far
more than his blind sister and widowed mother
would ever need for the rest of their lives. The sight
of it almost took his breath away.

'There ye are!' said the leprechaun. 'Would I try t' cheat ye? Now put me down and go and get something to dig it up with.'

The man's eyes narrowed, for he suspected that the leprechaun might be tricking him. 'And as soon as I set you down and go for a shovel, you'll move the treasure somewhere else,' he said warily. 'I know your sort, my little maneen.'

The leprechaun merely snorted. 'I'll do nothing of the sort,' he said airily. 'Indeed, you have my word that I won't lay a finger on it. Now set me down.'

The man looked around him. Every tree in the grove was the same, and they all clustered darkly together. Even if the leprechaun didn't move the treasure, he seriously doubted that he'd ever find that particular tree again. This, of course, must be what the leprechaun was counting on!

He thought hard. Then he hit on a plan. Tearing a strip of cloth from his shirt, he tied it round the lowest branch of the tree.

'Do I have your word that you won't touch that marker, or take it down?' he demanded.

'By the Blessed St Patrick and all the holy saints, ye have my word that I won't so much as lay a finger on it!' promised the leprechaun.

This was a powerful oath, and it satisfied the leprechaun's captor. 'Very well!' he said, putting the leprechaun down on the ground. 'In return for your promise, I'll grant you your freedom.' And in the twinkling of an eye, the little man was gone into the bushes nearby and there wasn't a trace of him to be seen. Indeed, he was never seen in that district again.

The man rushed home to get a spade and a pick, in order to dig up the fortune. He was hardly gone more than half an hour and was soon back at the *stand of trees, ready for work.*

But when he got there, a great shock awaited him. The leprechaun had been busy, all right. Every tree in that particular stand had a strip of cloth tied to its lowest branch, and every strip was exactly the same!

Try as he might, the poor fellow couldn't distinguish one from the other, nor could he remember exactly where the original tree — the one with the fortune at its roots — had been. He dug in several places but always came away empty-handed. Eventually, he had to give up and go back home — his blind sister and aged mother would have to do without the wealth. And as he went, a sound followed him, like the cackling of a bird, hidden away in a bush. Just for a moment, he thought that it might be the leprechaun laughing at him.

Sometimes, leprechauns would use their immense wealth to entrap mortal souls. Not only would fairy money transform itself into dead leaves, acorns or ashes once the fairy influence had departed; accepting it could damn mortal souls to Hell. Consequently, some leprechauns who steadfastly hated humankind would try to force individuals to accept their coinage, in the hope that they would be so damned. Fairy money was sometimes slipped into ordinary change or given as a reward or payment for some service rendered. Money, therefore, should never be accepted from strangers, and each coin given as change should be thoroughly checked. To ignore this warning could have extremely grave consequences.

The notion of the leprechaun trying to send human souls to Hell closely allies the fairy with the Devil (see Chapter Six, 'Leprechauns and Religion'). Rather than being a jolly, drunken, mischievous sprite, the fairy becomes the agent of dark supernatural powers and the enemy of all right-living people.

Although he is primarily portrayed as a cobbler, then, the leprechaun has a number of professions within the fairy world, some of which impinge on the mortal world. He is, in effect, a jack of all trades; and with the weight of such responsibility on his shoulders, he might perhaps be forgiven for his drunkenness and for his surly moods. With such a complicated portfolio, after all, he might be described, in modern-day terms, as being one of the real captains of industry in the fairy world.

Chapter Five

Leprechaun Society

Although they often give the appearance of being extremely shambolic and haphazard in their ways, leprechauns are exceptionally well-organised. And, although folklorists such as Yeats have classified them as solitary fairies, this organisation is predominantly a social one.

Generally speaking, leprechauns are organised into clan-groupings which have existed almost since the dawn of time and which were certainly established long before the first humans arrived in Ireland. The initial groupings are thought to have followed a rough north-south divide; but as the fairy (and leprechaun) population began to expand, these divisions became much more complicated.

Although no one is altogether certain, it is thought that there are four major clans within the leprechaun world, roughly corresponding to the four provinces of Ireland — Ulster, Munster, Leinster and Connaught. To these may be added the clan-grouping of Meath, which

was also an ancient province – the lands of the High
King at Tara. Within these clan-groupings there are a
number of sub-groupings, but little information on any
of these exists. The areas which these minor clans
inhabit are equivalent to ancient Irish *tuaths* (petty
kingdoms or pieces of land held by petty lords for their
overall ruler) and are subject to the domination of the
larger clans.

Even though very little research has been done on
the subject, it is generally assumed that each major clan
displays its own unique characteristics, which distinguish it
from the others. It is worth examining these characteristics, in order to explore the rich diversity which exists
in the leprechaun world.

Ulster leprechauns (laughremen) are believed to be
the finest storytellers and poets in the fairy world. They
have a command of words and imagery which is
unequalled anywhere else in Ireland. However, many of
their poems and songs are both lengthy and complicated.
The great eighteenth-century leprechaun poet Michaeleen
O'Coinn, from Slieve Gullion in South Armagh, is said
to have composed a work in honour of the harvest
which ran to 14,401 verses and took four days and
nights to recite in its entirety. Indeed, so complicated
was the verse and meter construction of the poem that
it could not be memorised or properly recited by any
mortal tongue, but only by that of a fairy. It is also said
that the famous bards of Armagh were initially trained
by leprechaun poets, and that this gave them their
great reputation for the imagery and sweetness of their
verse.

Many of the Ulster poems were set to music, and the
melodies are so beautiful that they were partly copied
by mortals from all over Ireland. Unfortunately, they
have long been lost. A similar situation exists in relation
to a number of other ancient tunes which are attributed

to the fairy folk: the original texts which accompanied many of these melodies no longer exist, and in most cases, mortal words have been added to the tune.

In spite of their reputation for beautiful words and melodies, Ulster leprechauns are amongst the most aggressive and factious fairies in Ireland. They are incredibly protective of the great wealth which they store — which is said to derive from the old kings of Ulster — and they usually suspect that everyone is trying to cheat them out of it. This makes them incredibly defensive and antisocial. They are also reputedly the strongest of all the leprechaun tribes and are terrific sportsmen, excelling at hurling (a favourite leprechaun sport) and football. Undoubtedly, their natural aggressive tendencies add to their fierce and uncompromising competitiveness.

They are also distinctive in their style of dress, often wearing conical or pointed hats as opposed to the soft, wide-brimmed hats worn by other leprechauns. This gives them a malignant and slightly sinister air which they seem to relish. Some leprechauns in South Armagh do not wear clothing at all; instead, they are covered with a wiry fur, through which their rather wizened faces peer, displaying sharp fang-like teeth. These fairies should not be approached under any circumstances. North Antrim grogochs have already been discussed; they are relatively friendly, but even they can turn nasty if a mortal crosses them. Although they are frequently spotted around riverbanks and under hedges, Ulster leprechauns are probably best avoided.

Connaught leprechauns have a reputation for being the most serious and academic of all their kind. While this may be only a rumour, they are said to be highly sober and industrious, spending most of their free time in scholarly study. In fact, it is said that the most notable of Connaught fairies do not drink at all — which is difficult to believe, given the inherent nature of the leprechaun.

These leprechauns are the shyest and most mystical of all the fairy folk. They are seen only infrequently, and then only by those who cannot harm them ('innocents', very small children and the seriously drunk). They are very conservative in their ways and shun the colourful dress of their counterparts in other provinces, preferring to clothe themselves in drab hues. They are said to wear plain brown or grey jerkins with cowls, which they often pull over their heads to hide most of their faces, making them look rather like monks. Their specialities are philosophy and literature. They are closely connected with trees, and are often to be seen amongst the roots of great oaks, absorbed in copying out some book or manuscript.

Their most striking feature is their long beards, which are symbolic of their great age and wisdom − the longer the beard, the wiser and more sagacious the leprechaun. Indeed, some of their beards are so long that they can easily be tucked into the leather belts which these fairies wear.

Connaught sprites are also said to be deeply interested in art, and can be quite artistic themselves when the mood takes them. Examples of their work − usually in the form of indecipherable and wholly abstract paintings − can be found as part of the mosses on some trees, or in the strange whorls of the trees themselves.

Probably because of their mystical characteristics, Connaught leprechauns are the most secretive of all their kind, choosing to inhabit lonely and inaccessible places − much like the early Christian Fathers. To see one, therefore, is something of a rarity.

Leinster leprechauns appear to be the sept upon which the common caricature of the leprechaun is based. They are easily the most drunken of all the species. They dress bizarrely, usually in clashing colours that make them stand out against any background. Consequently, these are the fairies which are most easily seen by mortals.

They are intensely fond of pranks and spend many of their nights letting out farmers' cattle, overturning their hayricks or committing other such rogueries about their property. They are inveterate liars, and nothing which they say must be believed, nor must any of their oaths be accepted.

Despite their wild and raucous ways, these are the most prosperous leprechauns in all of Ireland. It is estimated that these Leinster fairies have a total of sixteen million pounds hidden away in various locations across the province. Much of this money came from the coffers of the Norman barons who were invited into Ireland by Dermot MacMurrough, King of Leinster, during the twelfth century. Their treasure was hidden away in castles and monastic ruins, and all of these sites are known to the leprechauns of Leinster. Such wealth makes them especially defensive towards humans (and even towards other fairies), and they are generally regarded as the most tricky of all their kind in Ireland — some folklorists might say that they are the trickiest sprites in the whole of the Celtic world.

Leinster leprechauns claim to be the oldest family of their kind in Ireland, and there is no doubt that the original leprechauns came from somewhere within the province. However, this does not excuse their outlandish behaviour, and they are generally regarded with a kind of disdain by many other leprechaun septs, and by many other fairies right across the Irish countryside. Not that this upsets them; indeed, it seems to make them even more rowdy and boisterous in their ways. Leinster leprechauns are widely regarded as the 'rebels' of the fairy world, deliberately defying almost every form of generally accepted convention. Perhaps because of their inordinate wealth, they are generally tolerated by other fairies and are widely sought after by greedy mortals.

Meath leprechauns are well-known for their arrogance and snobbery. Although Leinster leprechauns claim to be the oldest of their species in Ireland, this is hotly disputed by the Meath fraternity, who claim that they and they alone are the oldest. Furthermore, they claim many connections with the old High Kings of Ireland, who had their seat at Tara, even though there is no real historical evidence for such claims. This, however, does not prevent the Meath leprechauns from putting on as many airs and graces as though they themselves were royalty.

They have a high opinion of themselves as diplomats, and claim to have interceded in many disputes in ancient Ireland — although this is certainly open to question. They also place a high value on their own eloquence and lay claim to several old ballads and poems which are more properly attributable to their Ulster brethren. They are widely known (and abhorred) for their ability to give long and convoluted speeches at the drop of a hat. They are also extremely curious, to the point of nosiness, and will often involve themselves in affairs which are not properly their concern. They will dispense advice which they claim has been 'culled from the centuries', but which is actually little more than their own overblown opinions.

They frequently set themselves up as arbitrators and mediators in disputes between other fairy folk, relying on their own 'great wisdom' to settle arguments. In many instances, such 'mediation' fails and the Meath leprechauns resort to age-old strategies — beating both parties into submission with a cudgel, or holding a knife to the throat of one of the parties in order to force him to make peace with the other. This is what counts as 'diplomacy'.

Unlike most other leprechauns, the Meath fraternity do not drink poteen with any frequency, preferring either mead or honey beer, which they consider a 'grand drink' and consume with great gusto. The fact that this drink has its origins amongst the English Saxons does not appear to deter them, and they have been known to quaff copious amounts of English ale with similar relish, claiming that it was a drink of the ancient High Kings of Ireland (this is without question erroneous).

Their clothing is much finer and slightly more colour-coordinated than that of their counterparts elsewhere, and this is taken as a sign that they consider themselves to be the 'aristocrats' of the leprechaun world. However, like any other leprechaun's, their word is not to be trusted; and, given the slightest opportunity, they will resort to mischievous tricks and pranks, just like others of their species.

Munster leprechauns are thieves, ruffians and robbers. It is often said that they give their Leinster relatives a run for their money when it comes to drinking, but this may be simply boasting on the part of some Munster folklorists. Munster leprechauns are the ones who are most likely to come into contact with humans, since they frequently break into houses in order to steal whatever they can, eat whatever food has been left untouched and consume whatever drink happens to be available. It is amongst these fairies that the highest incidence of cluricauns is to be found (see Chapter Seven).

These leprechauns are famed for their fast thinking and their way with words. They are generally regarded as the sweetest talkers in Ireland, with the ability to charm the fowls out of the air through the power of their words. Conchabhar Thadhg MacRúairí of Clare, the great hedge-poet, allegedly learned his skill with words from a Munster leprechaun, as did the wandering poet from County Cavan, Cahal Buí. (It is said that he also acquired his fondness for strong drink from the leprechaun.) Another Clare poet, Brian Merriman, is also said to have been greatly influenced by the Munster sprites. It is well-known that Munster fairies also have a penchant for exaggerated stories, particularly those regarding themselves. They will portray themselves as great warriors or scholars, with such skill that their listeners will totally believe them and will be gripped by the tales of their fictitious exploits.

These fairies are inveterate gamblers and will wager on anything — even upon two flies climbing a wall or upon the length of a shadow at midday. Many of the fairy fairs and goblin markets throughout Munster have some games of chance; passing mortals can be drawn to these and persuaded to part with their money. Even if a Munster leprechaun should lose at one of these activities, he is so skilful with words that he can usually escape paying out what he has lost and may even manage to persuade his opponent that it is he who has lost the wager.

The Munster leprechauns are reputed to be fine musicians and exceptionally sweet singers — although there is no evidence for such a claim. Indeed, many folklorists claim that they are in fact the worst musicians and singers in the fairy realm, and possibly in all of Ireland (although they are believed to be reasonable dancers), and that they put all their undoubted artistry into talk and blarney.

It is also said that they are amongst the few of the leprechaun tribe who will actually marry mortal women. However, marriage to a Munster leprechaun is not to be sought, for they, like all leprechauns, are extremely untrustworthy and flighty in their ways. No good can ever come of such unions. It is advisable, given their roguery and wild ways, that Munster leprechauns should be utterly avoided, even though they are the most accessible of the leprechaun species.

Beyond these admittedly sweeping classifications, not very much is known about organisation within the Irish leprechaun world. There are known to be a large number of smaller septs and groups, but the leprechauns remain very secretive about how they are structured and about their exact functions. It is not even known if they are established along family or kinship lines; but, since many leprechauns appear to bear different names, this seems extremely unlikely. In Scotland, the situation is thought to be slightly different: leprechauns may be organised along lines similar to those of the Highland clans, by connections of family and kin. However, no hard evidence exists for this assumption, which is mainly based upon hearsay and folk-tale.

In Ireland, there are some hints which lead to certain deductions regarding the structure of leprechaun groupings. For example, each sept (no matter how minor) has a leader, generally known as 'Himself', who is the most prominent leprechaun in a given locality. Every four to five years, these local leaders are required to swear allegiance' to an overlord of the entire Irish leprechaun nation — 'the Grand Himself'.

Another name for the leader (both national and local) is 'Ferganainm', which literally means 'man without a name'. In ancient Ireland, this title was used amongst the Gaelic aristocracy to denote illegitimacy — certain Irish clan leaders, including Ferganainm O'Carroll and Ferganainm O'Neill, used it as a proper name — but folklorists believe that amongst the fairy kind it may mean something altogether different. It seems, in fact, to be a title of high rank.

We do not know how often the Grand Himself (or Ferganainm) changes, or how his successor is chosen, although it is thought that this might be either by popular vote or by some great feat — such as drinking a barrel of poteen at one sitting.

The loyalty-swearing by the various lower Himselfs is reminiscent of the ancient Ard Feis, during which sub-chieftains swore their allegiance to the Ard Rí (High King) of Ireland in former times. Like this great festival, the loyalty-swearing ceremony takes place over four or five days, during which there is much merriment and a great deal of strong drink is consumed.

The pattern of the festivities is determined by the locality in which the event takes place. If, for instance, the ceremony is held in Ulster, then it is characterised by a great hurling match and by various feats of strength and physical skill. If it is held in Connaught (and few of them are), then it will be characterised by debate, recitation and the composing of poetry. It has even been noted (although not verified) that some Connaught gatherings are completely 'dry' — i.e. devoid of any form of strong drink: the leprechauns there declare that poetry should be 'sufficient liquor to intoxicate the soul'.

Should the ceremony be held in Munster, its main attraction will be the lies and tall stories of the participants, while those ceremonies held in Leinster (where the majority of them are, in fact, held) are usually no more than drunken brawls. Leinster and Munster gatherings also tend to be marketplaces where 'mislaid' property — usually stolen from the homes of mortals — is on sale, games of chance abound, and there is trading, bargaining and wagering in abundance. In these cases, the swearing of loyalty to the Grand Himself usually takes second place or is even forgotten about altogether (as, according to some stories told by old people in Munster, it was in 1897, 1902 and 1931).

The grandest gatherings are, as might be expected, held by the leprechauns of Meath. Although these are not always strictly leprechaun functions (other fairies, and sometimes the occasional mortal — assuming that he or she is of sufficiently high status — are occasionally invited to attend them), they epitomise the genteel side of the fairy world. Such occasions, according to other leprechauns, are very 'boring', filled with lofty conversations and frequent name-dropping, with none of the drunken jollity which characterises the gatherings in some other provinces. These gatherings are normally shunned by the Ulster, Munster and Leinster leprechauns, with the Connaught contingent only making a token appearance.

Although all these meetings (which are supposed to be formal ceremonies) have a haphazard air about them, it is well-known that leprechauns are fiercely loyal, both to their sept and to their province. If called upon to perform any task for the local Himself or the Grand Himself, each leprechaun will obey without question. It is inherent in their nature to do so, and this gives a form of structure to their entire society.

In the early days, it is said, there were frequent wars and battles between various septs (and even provinces) of leprechauns, during which local Himselfs called upon their followers to fight for the honour of their localities. Old people will still speak about seeing so-called 'fairy fights', either in the sky or in remote places, during which great armies of leprechauns faced each other. The sheer numbers involved speak eloquently of how readily such calls to arms were heeded. Nowadays, although times are much more peaceful in the fairy world, leprechaun leaders still inspire (and demand) almost unquestioning loyalty from those below them.

LepRechaun Law

With any form or organised structure comes the concept
of law, and the leprechauns are no different in this
respect. Like the ancient Brehon laws of Ireland and the
Laws of Hywel Dda in Wales, leprechaun laws are not
thought to be written down in any coherent or cohesive
whole. Nor is there really any unifying principle which
defines these laws, since most of them are communally
based, pertaining to the specific community in which
they are used. It is extremely doubtful whether any of
them are actually written down; if they are, it is unlikely
that they are transcribed in any codes or books. If they
do exist, it is in a scattered and fragmented form which
is not readily accessible either to mortals or, indeed, to
the leprechauns themselves. Much of their law, it is
suspected, exists only on an *ad hoc* or localised basis.

Most laws are enacted through a tribunal of judges or
'casters' (no doubt they take this title from the financial
arbiters at human fairs — especially rabbit fairs — and
markets right across Ireland). The chairman of such
tribunals is usually, although not necessarily, a local
Himself. The tribunal may comprise the three oldest
leprechauns in any given community, but it is more
probable that in some areas the members are chosen by
the drawing of lots.

On some occasions, the casters at a court consist of
leprechauns from another locality or province. For
example, leprechauns in Ulster may be tried by a tribunal
from Munster, and vice versa. Leprechauns from Meath
consider themselves to be great and impartial judges,
although this is open to question. They are brought in to
sit in a number of fairy courts, though this probably has
more to do with their self-perceived high status than
with any formal legal expertise. Because of their
knowledge of ancient texts and their inherent wisdom

and good sense, Connaught leprechauns are much sought after as casters, though the majority of them decline the honour. Few Connaught leprechauns become involved in anything legal; on the whole, they prefer to study things like history and philosophy.

Tribunals are convened only when there is some sort of dispute between leprechauns, or when it is alleged that some sort of crime has been committed. (These are not 'crimes' in the human sense; they may include excessive noisiness, long periods of relative sobriety, and so on.) The casters will hear all sides and will deliberate at length (usually over copious amounts of poteen, supplied by the local leprechaun community) before arriving at their decision. This judgement does not have to be unanimous — a simple majority verdict will do.

From the (admittedly questionable) accounts of those mortals who have secretly witnessed them, leprechaun courts seem to be rather undisciplined affairs, reminiscent of courtrooms in the American Wild West. Strong drink is permitted to be served throughout the proceedings, and this often leads to rowdy and undisciplined behaviour amongst both the spectators and the judges. Indeed, it is said that on a number of occasions, during certain lengthy proceedings, the judges became so intoxicated that they could not reach a coherent decision. There is also, if reports are to be believed, a great deal of trading and selling amongst leprechauns within the court, so the whole affair takes on the appearance of a market.

The casters sit at the head of the courtroom, which is usually an open area in the corner of a field, or a ruined building which has been specially designated for this purpose. The chairman of the tribunal carries with him a bachall, or staff, which is suggestive of the ancient Irish Brehons or druids. This is the symbol of his authority in the situation, and he will not deliver his judgement without it.

There are no lawyers; petitioners are simply called to state their cases, whilst the tribunal frequently refreshes itself with liquor as it gives due consideration to their pleas. Each petitioner may, if he chooses, bring a number of supporters to urge him on and to add due weight to his case. They are permitted to call out encouragement to those whom they support, and to ridicule the opposition as they see fit. If things get a bit out of hand, Himself is permitted to beat rowdy participants about the ears with his bachall in order to quieten them down. However, neither Himself nor the casters will be averse to a little bribery, and they are equally vulnerable to intimidation, which may produce a similar result.

The judgements issued by leprechaun courts usually involve fines and compensations. Since leprechauns are usually very protective of the wealth that they have stored away, this is a serious deterrent against bad behaviour; and if the case is a dispute between two sprites, this usually brings about a speedy agreement. In some cases, the head of the tribunal has the right to batter both wrongdoers and disputants about the skulls with his bachall. In cases of dispute or bad behaviour, the severity of the judgement is also dependent upon the temperaments and idiosyncrasies of the casters, although certain general principles are usually observed. Crimes of mischief against mortals, for example, are not considered to be crimes at all, since most leprechauns regard mortals as slow and stupid, whereas crimes against the fairy population — a leprechaun being excessively rowdy and making a nuisance of himself, for example — are often regarded with the utmost severity.

Since leprechauns are immortal, there is no death penalty under fairy law (for fairies, that is; these courts can pass the death sentence upon mortals — see below).

The most dire penalties which a leprechaun court can issue consist of 'being sent to Coventry' (i.e. being shut out of all normal fairy relationships and being treated with disdain and silence) or, in the most extreme cases, expulsion and exile from the local community. For a leprechaun, banishment to another locality where he knows no one is equivalent to a long gaol sentence. These sanctions, it has to be said, are not very often used; but when they are, they are used to great effect. A similar draconian judgement entails depriving the leprechaun of his distilling equipment and forcing him to be 'dry' (without liquor of any description) for a specified period.

It should be noted that leprechaun law differs from human law in that, once Himself and his casters have made their judgement, there is no appeal against it. In order to formalise things, the chairman of the tribunal will strike his bachall on the ground, exclaiming loudly, 'It is so.' The judgement of the leprechaun court is then immutably fixed.

Leprechaun courts will sometimes pass judgement on humans, particularly if they have committed some slight against the fairies − cutting down a fairy thorn, crossing a fairy path without permission, destroying a fairy rath or showing disrespect in some other form. Leprechauns consider themselves to be the protectors of the land (they are, after all, supposed to be the manifestations of the ancient land gods of Ireland) and therefore claim jurisdiction over those who despoil it. The penalties which their courts impose upon mortals can be extremely severe − utter bankruptcy, twisted limbs or spines, illness, and sometimes even a painful and lingering death. For humans, as for fairies, there is no appeal against the judgement of the court.

Although quite detailed descriptions of leprechaun courts have been given above, very little is actually known about their system of justice (if, in fact, such a concept exists amongst them). Indeed, it is generally thought that the formal gatherings described are not called very often, and that when they are, they are not in session for very long. No record of leprechaun law has ever been found, and therefore much of our 'knowledge' of it consists largely of speculation. Nevertheless, it is still wise to say 'By your leave' when crossing a known fairy path, and to leave fairy bushes well alone, lest the full force of the leprechaun legislature fall upon your shoulders.

Chapter Six

Leprechauns and Religion

When it comes to ghosts and fairies, the Church has sometimes found itself in an invidious and confusing position. It could not very well deny the existence of supernatural creatures, since that might also be to deny that there were evil forces such as demons; but it could not fully acknowledge them, either. Furthermore, in many isolated rural areas, old folk beliefs still lingered on; and it was perhaps better to partially acknowledge the existence of sprites and spirits, and to bring them under religious control, than to have them still secretly worshipped by a local populace, in defiance of Church strictures.

Since a number of ancient texts declared fairies to be the last remnants of the old pagan land gods, the Church in the main was quick to denounce them (and leprechauns in particular) as the servants of the dark powers, closely associated with the Devil himself. However, some religious teaching stated that they were fallen angels who would never see Paradise again. This placed them at variance with God and the gradually developing notion of Heaven within the holy mind. No fairy, the Church firmly stated, could enter the heavenly gates.

In fact, Church teaching decreed that no supernatural being could enter Heaven unless he or she had at least some connection to humanity, for whom Christ died. The most common test was to ask the being if he or she had 'but one drop of Adam's blood' in his or her veins. The majority of fairies could not claim this, and so were excluded from the human afterlife. Leprechauns were included amongst the supernatural throng who were shut out of Heaven, as this old tale from County Down, collected from the great storyteller W.J. Fitzpatrick in 1953, affirms.

Just beyond Moneydarragh School, there was an old priest living at one time. He had been the serving priest in the locality, but he was long retired, although he continued to live around Moneydarragh. His name was Priest O'Hagan, and he was very well-liked and very highly respected by the people round about. He was also extremely wise on all things religious, and the country people still came to him if they had a problem or if they were in trouble. He would always give them a hearing.

The house that he lived in was a large place, set in its own grounds, that belonged to his family. As Priest O'Hagan grew older, he couldn't manage the place the same way that he used to, and so he employed a serving man called Ned to work about the house and to do odd jobs for him.

One evening Ned was working around the back of the place, where the fields ran down into the priest's garden. There was a big standing stone set into a low bank, just on the very edge of the grounds, which was supposed to be badly fairy-haunted. The local people would give it a wide berth, but it never bothered Priest O'Hagan, him being a man of the cloth and all. He was content to let it stand. 'It'll be standing here long after I'm in the clay,' he used to say.

The sun was going down behind the Mourne Mountains, and Ned was just clearing away the last of the day's work from around the big stone. The shadows were lengthening, and he was uneasy about working there, but he wanted to have everything finished before he went home. Priest O'Hagan was in the house, eating his own supper, and Ned dearly wanted to be by his fireside, doing the same thing.

All of a sudden, he had the feeling that he was being watched; and, turning suddenly, he saw some-one standing close beside the big standing stone — so close, in fact, that the figure almost seemed to be a part of the stone itself. It was a little man — no bigger than a three-year-old child — with a long skirty coat which reached almost to the ground and a soft, wide-brimmed hat which threw most of his face into shadow. Ned, however, was aware of his eyes, which watched him with a frightful intensity.

There was one other thing about him which made poor Ned's blood freeze. Even in the last rays of the sun, which fell full across the ground, the little man cast no shadow!

Ned knew then that his visitor was one of the leprechauns who were supposed to dwell beside the large stone. He moved to make the sign of the Cross in the air, to ward away evil, but his hand simply would not obey him.

'W-what is it that you want from me?' asked Ned, his voice trembling badly.

The little man paused for a moment. 'I want you

to ask the priest a question,' he answered. 'For it is said that he is extremely wise on religious matters.'

Ned relaxed a little, but he was still wary. He knew that leprechauns could be extremely tricky creatures and were always anxious to entrap mortal souls.

'He is indeed,' he answered, a bit more confidently. 'There is none wiser on such things in the whole of Ireland. But you can ask him yourself. He is in the house beyond, having his supper.'

The little man cast a long glance towards the house. 'I would if I could,' he replied. 'But I fear the collar about his neck and the stink of his holy incense offend me.'

In Ned's mind, this confirmed that the being to whom he spoke was indeed a leprechaun.

'Will you ask him a question for me?' the other persisted.

Ned swallowed. 'I will, right gladly,' he said at last, not wishing to offend the leprechaun for fear of some reprisal. 'But Priest O'Hagan is a kind man and will not harm you, no matter who you might be.'

'He is still a priest!' retorted the little man. 'But since you agree to ask the question, it is this: is there any hope of salvation for me? Ask him if I will ever see the delightful mansions which are said to lie in Paradise. Will you do that for me?'

'I will,' replied Ned, still fearful of the other.

'Then I'll come back at the same time tomorrow evening, and you can give me his answer,' said the little man.

And even as he spoke, a bird called in a nearby field, high and shrill, and Ned involuntarily turned to look in its direction. And when he turned his head back again, he was alone beside the big standing stone.

He went into the house and found Priest O'Hagan
finishing his supper, a holy book propped up on the
table in front of him. Ned explained about his meeting
with the little man and how the leprechaun had
wanted to ask the priest a question.

'What did he want to ask me?' asked the old man,
with great kindness in his voice.

Ned told him the question, and Priest O'Hagan
thought for a long while without ever saying a word.
At last he spoke again.

'I do not truly know the answer to his question,'
he said, 'but you can tell him this: if he has so much
as one drop of Adam's blood in his veins, then he has
as much hope of salvation as any man. But if he has
not, then salvation is denied to him and he will
never see Paradise. That is all I can tell him.' And
Ned left the old man to his reading.

The next evening, he was finishing his work again,
close to the big stone, when he had the feeling that
he was being watched once more. Turning swiftly, he
saw the little man standing amongst the late-evening
shadows close to the stone. Ned's heart nearly
stopped within him; but, swallowing, he stepped
forward to meet his visitor.

'Well,' said the leprechaun, without any sort of
greeting, 'did you ask him?'

'I did,' replied Ned.

'And what did he say?'

'He said that he truly didn't know the answer to
your question, but he would tell you this: if you have
only a drop of Adam's blood in your veins, you will
have as much chance of salvation as any man; but
if you don't, then salvation is not for you and you
will never see Paradise at all. That was all he could
tell you.'

For a moment, the little man looked fixedly at

Ned, as if taking in his words; then he crouched down and gave a long, long cry of great sadness. 'Ochone! Ochone!' His weeping would have broken your heart to hear it.

At the sound of his cry, a hare started up in the field nearby and went flashing over the grass. Instinctively, Ned turned his head to see it go; and when he turned back, he was alone again. There was nothing there except the big stone, casting its shadow in the late-evening sun.

As they were to be denied the pleasures of Paradise by virtue of the fact that they had no human blood in their veins, fairies and leprechauns were continually trying to find ways of getting around the prohibition. We have already noted that fairy women who had children by mortal men were always trying to get these babies baptised in the Christian Church, in order that they might attain the afterlife. Since many of these children are thought to have been leprechauns, it is reasonable to suppose that many leprechauns had hopes of immortality through some sort of Christian immersion. For example, because many baptismal fonts were situated close to the entrances of churches, it was believed that leprechauns sometimes concealed themselves close to the doorways of country churches to catch any of the sacred baptismal water which might be spilled, so that they themselves might be baptised in the Christian manner. Similarly, it was believed that the crumbs of the sacred Host would attract leprechauns who wished to partake of it in the hope of attaining some form of salvation. Nevertheless, the Church stated that they had no souls and therefore could not receive divine grace, or else that they were so wicked and pagan that God had turned His face from them.

'It was said that the leprechauns of Ireland and the

other wee folk of the fairy world would never see Heaven,' said the great Limerick storyteller Kate Ahern. 'But that didn't prevent them from stopping every passing clergyman and asking him if there was any way they could get there. The answer was always the same: if they had even one spot of human blood, they might see Paradise. Not one of them had, and you could hear their cries and lamentations in every old rath and fort all across Ireland. It was a long, low sound, like the wind in the bushes, but it was the cry of the leprechauns that had been denied God's salvation.'

Leprechauns and Exorcism

Because leprechauns were often considered to be either servants or actual emanations of the Devil himself, it was essential that the Church should demonstrate its power over them. The way in which it showed its authority over demons and evil presences was through exorcism, and this practice was deemed to apply to leprechauns and the fairy kind as well.

As pagan and Christian myth fused into a generalised folklore, it was widely believed that the very sight of a priest or clergyman could put leprechauns to flight. As is implied in the above story, leprechauns were greatly frightened even of being in the same room as a man of the cloth. The holiness which he exuded was considered to be anathema to the leprechauns (who were, after all, pagan deities) and would invariably drive them out, even without any form of ritual being performed.

However, as folklore developed and became slightly more complex, the mere presence of a holy man was not considered to be enough. Some form of religious rite — a blessing, or the celebration of mass — had to be performed before the leprechauns would leave. There are even tales of leprechauns laughing and mocking the priests and reverend gentlemen who came to expel them from a site. Certainly, in many of the later tales (from around the last century) the leprechauns showed no fear of holy men *per se*. Even the sight of a bishop did not deter them.

The clergymen, therefore, had to recite some form of exorcism in order to rid any site of fairies and leprechauns. The most popular was the rite for driving away demons and ghosts, since, by the mid-to-late 1800s, these had become connected with leprechauns in the popular mind. The phrase 'leprechaun-haunted' or 'fairy-haunted' was beginning to creep into the vernacular tongue — the word 'haunted' signifying a strong association with ghosts or phantoms.

How could one assess whether or not an exorcism was called for? This judgement was usually based upon both the level and the intent of the leprechaun activities involved. Leprechauns, as we have said, are by nature mischievous creatures, continually playing tricks and pranks upon unsuspecting mortals. It appears that some leprechauns ventured beyond mere mischief and into the realms of actual malevolence. It was against these sprites that the Church extended its power through the holy rite of exorcism.

The 'malevolence' which the leprechauns showed towards humankind could take many forms. They could, for example, pelt individuals with stones, rocks and other objects as they walked around their property; they could cause burning peats to fall from the fireplace, injuring both humans and animals; they could sing bawdy songs, or disclose scandalous things concerning visitors to a house, from secret locations around the rooms (for example, from the chimney); they could break windows and cause hideous apparitions to appear; they could pinch and scratch children as they lay asleep, or cause their beds to levitate alarmingly.

In many ways, leprechaun malevolence paralleled what we would now describe as poltergeist activity. Descriptions of flaming coals flying around the room and of plates leaping from a dresser to be broken on the floor, which seem to be common features of poltergeist phenomena, also match descriptions of leprechaun malevolence towards humans. The Rev. St John Seymour, a clergyman who had an interest in the supernatural, mentions an incident in Larne, County Antrim, in 1710, in which leprechauns at a rath near the town invisibly bombarded passers-by with stones and foul matter. And the tormenting of the elderly Mrs Hattridge (Haltridge), which began the Islandmagee witch trial in the same county, was initially ascribed to leprechauns who were supposed to dwell nearby. In this instance, the movement, in the popular mind, from leprechauns to witches shows how closely the fairies were identified with the powers of evil.

'Malevolence' amongst leprechauns could also include diverting the pure in heart from thinking on sacred things. For instance, an old story from Limerick describes how, one sunny afternoon, a country priest dozed in the sunshine with his breviary on his lap, and how the leprechauns came and stole the holy book from out of his hands. On awakening, the priest, realising what had been done, cursed them all in God's name, turning them into stones and rocks. This demonstrated the power of the clergy over the pagan sprites. Similarly, many nuns complained of leprechauns pinching them during mass in order to make them angry and uncomfortable during the Holy Sacrament. Again, this is a clear link with demons and devils.

Formal rituals, involving both pagan and Christian elements, were often performed to drive out leprechauns and other supernatural nuisances. The most complete description which we have of such a ritual comes from the townland of Derryork in North Derry, and is recounted in the Ordnance Survey Memoirs for the 1830s. A weaver, Joseph MacPhearson, was plagued with leprechauns and other fairy folk from a nearby rath, who interrupted his work with their merriment. He went to plead with them to be quiet, but they only became more rowdy, and in time they actually invaded his house. He could not get near his loom for the number of leprechauns who were partying in his front room.

In desperation, he called the local clergyman, who arrived bearing a Bible and carrying an iron knife — the knife embodies the ancient superstition that all fairies (and leprechauns in particular) feared the metal, which has been regarded, since before recorded history, as having magical properties. Placing the knife across the open pages of Scripture, the minister (who appears to have been a Protestant) read an Office of Exorcism and dispelled the leprechauns from the dwelling.

The exorcism, however, seems to have been largely ineffective: the following night, the leprechauns were back again and almost set the house on fire through their carelessness. Many of the locals claimed that it was because a Protestant minister had been brought in — had a Catholic priest delivered the exorcism, it would have had greater effect. Later the leprechauns were to refer derisively to 'Joe MacPhearson's leaves and lances' (the pages of Scripture and the iron knife) in their taunting of the poor weaver.

There are also some references to exorcisms carried out by Catholic priests to expel leprechauns from ruined or abandoned churches, or other holy precincts, in which they had taken up residence. In east Tipperary, for example, near the famous (and fairy-haunted) Slievenamon, a rite of exorcism was carried out in order to drive out leprechauns from a ruined church. However, details of the actual ritual are extremely vague, and there is no indication of whether it was successful or not. As time went on, however, leprechauns seem to have become more resistant to the banishments of the Church, and rituals against them appear to have been — on the surface, at least — largely ineffectual.

But it was not only buildings and sites that needed Church exorcism. Sometimes people might be possessed as well. Some leprechauns were said to be so small that they could hide themselves amongst greenery such as lettuce or cabbage, so that mortals inadvertently ate them in salads or stews. They then took possession of the mortal's body, causing it to perform acts which it would not normally do.

Added to this, leprechaun malevolence could extend to influencing those who were especially holy, making them do things which were completely out of character. Those who ate with the leprechauns, or who were overly friendly or deferential towards them, were especially at risk.

Sometimes those who refused to do their bidding were equally in jeopardy. St John Seymour notes the seventeenth-century case of Lord Ossery's butler (apparently a Sligo man), who refused to play a game of cards with the leprechauns; he then had to barricade himself in his house all day, 'for fear of being possessed by them'. When he did eventually set foot outside the door, he was thrown about and dragged out into the fields by some invisible power. He was brought for exorcism to the great Puritan divine, Valentine Greatrakes (the Irish Stroker), under whose eyes he was levitated into the air and suffered great and frequent fits of various sorts under the influence of the leprechauns. A 'friendly spirit' later told him to drink the juice of plantain roots to cure himself of one sort of fit, but informed him that he would have to suffer other fits and seizures — and be borne about at the whim of the invisible company of leprechauns — for the rest of his life. The spirit added that if the butler had 'acknowledged God in all his ways', he would not have been subject to the fairy power.

In fact, it was widely believed in many rural areas that committing sin invited leprechauns and other fairy-creatures to take control of one's life, in much the same way as it was believed that living a godless life encouraged evil to take possession of one's immortal soul. This certainly put the stamp of evil upon the fairies and the leprechauns, as part of the fairy world gradually came to be seen as undoubted servants of the Devil and implacable enemies of all godly people.

Leprechauns and the Dead

The cult of the dead was very strong amongst the ancient Celts and, perhaps, was particularly widespread in Ireland. The *Fáilte na Marbh* (Feast of the Dead — 31 October) took on a special resonance in northerly Celtic lands, where the winter days were dark and gloomy and the nights were cold and dark, suggestive of the nearness of the watchful dead. Naturally, this fascination with departed ancestors tinged fairy lore and gave it a more sinister edge.

Leprechauns, it was said, had been commanded by God to guard the souls of the dead and convey them to the gates of Heaven, which they themselves were not allowed to enter. This ritual was known in many country areas as 'the fairy funeral'. It concerned the spirits of those who had died within the preceding year. At certain times, when the veil between the mortal world and the afterlife was especially thin — such as

31 October, Hallowe'en — wandering souls which had been tied to the earth since their demise were rounded up and marched along darkened country roads under a leprechaun escort.

This was an especially dangerous time for travellers, for, should one chance to meet with the fairy funeral, the leprechauns had the power to take him or her with them into the afterlife, and the traveller's body would be found by the roadside the following morning. It was generally supposed, too, that the leprechauns would be in a particularly savage and unaccommodating mood at this time, having been forced by divine decree to approach the gates of Heaven without admission whilst mortals were allowed in. They were therefore especially likely to play malicious tricks upon whomever they met. Even to glance out of a window and see this supernatural cavalcade pass was to invite disaster. At worst, the watcher could be left blind or insane; at the very least, a bucket of blood might be dashed in his or her face. It was as well to stay in the house, keeping the doors and windows well-fastened and the curtains or shutters closed.

Nevertheless, there were those who, for one reason or another, braved the roads on nights when the fairy funeral was said to be abroad, and many stories about encounters with the eerie procession have passed into Irish country folklore. Margaret Gallagher, from outside the village of Belcoo in County Fermanagh, relates the following story concerning her grandfather, Pat Gallagher:

My grandfather was coming home one night from a céilí in Drumcully, beyond Belcoo, on the way to Garrison. He was coming round the roads when he met with the fairy funeral. He knew what it was, for he could hear the crying and wailing of those souls from the locality that the fairies were taking with them. He saw that there were a number of little men in long, long coats that were walking in front of the procession like undertakers at an ordinary funeral. He was greatly frightened and pulled himself up on the ditch so that they would pass him by.

Only he knew what to say, he would have been taken with them into the Beyond. He turned his coat inside out and said, 'My back from you, my face to you,' and they passed him by without seeing him at all. He always said that he had a very lucky escape, all right, for he could have been taken away with them.

Not all travellers on the night-time roads were as lucky as Pat Gallagher. There are plenty of stories of those who met with the fairy funerals and were carried off by the leprechauns, or were forced to perform some gruesome task before being returned to the mortal world. For instance, the traveller might have been forced to carry a coffin — or, worse, an unshrouded corpse — upon his back for the length of the entire night, or to some burial spot which the leprechauns had designated.

The story of the unfortunate Teig O'Kane from County Leitrim is well-known. Throughout the length of a Hallowe'en night, 'little men' forced poor Teig to stumble along gloomy, unlit roads and country lanes, carrying a dead body upon his shoulders, desperately trying to find some burial place for it. In the most common version of the story, the leprechauns whom he meets are described as being small, 'about the height of a child,' and dressed entirely in grey. They have 'a wicked way about them' and they are exceptionally violent towards Teig, kicking him and beating him with sticks. They are certainly no jolly cobblers, and this probably reflects the leprechauns' surly and envious attitude at this particular time of the year.

Some stories also mention that it was possible for certain mortals to remove the spirits of the recently dead from amongst the ghostly throng and bring them home again. To do this, the mortal had to outwit the leprechauns by using some sort of charm or spell (such as the incantation used by Pat Gallagher) which would render him or her invisible. (Hen-dung was considered a particularly effective 'charm' against the leprechauns who guarded the dead.) There are several tales of husbands whose wives had died (or appeared to have died), but who were able to snatch them back as the leprechauns passed by their doors. This reversal of death may have been connected with catalepsy, which often gave the victim a deathlike appearance, or with the temporary effects of some disease.

After any encounter with a leprechaun — or, indeed, any member of the fairy race — whether in a fairy funeral or not, it was considered advisable to attend mass as soon as possible. At the very least, one should consult and receive blessing from a priest. This was in case evil magic should somehow taint the individual and so damn his or her immortal soul. Alternatively, one could run home, fall upon one's knees and recite the Lord's Prayer, which would at least 'stay' the evil until mass could be observed. Sometimes a ritual of exorcism had to be said in the house in which the person who had met the leprechauns dwelt, lest he or she had somehow 'contaminated' the place with fairy magic.

The notion of leprechauns, then, harked back to the old pagan gods of the earth, and they were not fairies with whom the Church was especially comfortable. Despite their often jocular and mischievous ways and appearance, they were widely considered to be emanations of evil forces, to be widely avoided. It was considered advisable, therefore, to keep a crucifix or a holy medal about one's person or dwelling, in case one should encounter a leprechaun. When met with such religious artefacts or with holy prayers, it was said, the sprite would 'vanish away like the smoke from a chimney'. That was what the Church taught, at least!

Chapter Seven

The Leprechaun's Cousins:
Cluricauns and Sheela-na-Gigs

Cluricauns

It would be extremely remiss to conduct any discussion of the leprechaun without mentioning the cluricaun. Although many leprechauns deny all knowledge of such a being, or treat him with indifference or disdain, he is in fact closely related to them. In fact, some folklorists have described him as 'the leprechaun's first cousin'.

A fleeting reference to the cluricaun has already been made in connection with Munster leprechauns. Most cluricauns are to be found in Munster, although there are reports of them in other provinces as well. The cluricaun shares several of the leprechaun's characteristics; many who have seen both of them claim that it is often difficult to tell them apart.

The main differences between leprechauns and cluricauns are those of fashion and temperament. While the leprechaun pays little attention to dress and style, preferring mismatched clothing reminiscent of artisan garb, the cluricaun dresses in more flamboyant garments. While the leprechaun has a preference for subdued, natural shades (which will camouflage him much better out of doors), the cluricaun puts on more striking and gaudy colours, having a special affinity for red and plum hues. While the leprechaun closely resembles the artisan which he is supposed to be, the cluricaun has the air of a down-at-heel gentleman out on a spree. Although colourful, his clothing is rather shabby and dusty, patched with pieces of material of different shades. His shoes, though buckled, are often scuffed and worn, with the soles coming away from the uppers (something which deeply shocks even the most easy-going leprechaun).

The cluricaun's skin is much ruddier than that of the leprechaun (leprechauns are frequently believed to be slightly pallid), giving him a perpetually drunken appearance. Sometimes, although not always, he is inclined to be more hairy; and in contrast to leprechauns, who are mostly clean-shaven, he allows his beard to grow to a great length — on occasion, he can tuck it into his belt, in the fashion of Connaught leprechauns. Rather than smoking a dudeen, he is given to puffing upon a foul-smelling 'Danish pipe' (an old-fashioned, sometimes ornamented long-stemmed pipe), which he fills with some indefinable mixture.

While the leprechaun is industrious and surly, the cluricaun is idle but extremely cheery. Inordinately fond of strong drink, he resembles the sot who frequently props up the corner of the bar in public houses. Like many drunks, he regards himself as a bit of a dandy and irresistible to women, be they mortal or fairy.

The cluricaun is also a robber, stealing from mortal homes. While the household is asleep, he will break in and take what he can — usually drink or food. Through his magic, he will enter wine cellars or pantries, even locked cupboards, and help himself to whatever bottles of liquor he can find. This explains why the level of drink in some bottles seems to fall inexplicably over the course of a few nights. He will also gorge himself upon leftover pie or fowl, or whatever bread or potatoes he can find. Usually he will not take money, but he is attracted to shiny things and gaudy jewellery, which he will sometimes take away with him. When he has tired of these, he will sometimes (although not always) return them, hiding them in rather inaccessible places around the house — down the back of an armchair, or in some infrequently opened drawer. He is not malicious; he is more of a nuisance than anything else.

Cluricauns do not carry money, nor do they have any knowledge of hidden hoards of gold. They simply steal or take what they want with impunity. This sometimes makes them vulnerable to capture by vigilant mortals. If caught, however, the cluricaun can usually charm himself out of any situation, mainly by force of his cheery personality and his way with words. Should his captor's gaze be diverted, even for the briefest moment, then the cluricaun — like his leprechaun cousin — will vanish almost immediately. Consequently, if he is cornered, most of his admittedly pleasant conversation will be designed to divert and distract his captor so that he can escape.

There is no doubt that cluricauns are grand company. They are regarded as great storytellers and have a fount of old tales, stretching back into the mists of antiquity, which will astound and delight the listener. If cornered, the cluricaun will invariably suggest that his captor 'open a bottle' with him so that they can resolve the matter 'over a glass, like two civilised beings'. Here the mortal needs to be wary, for the cluricaun's capacity for strong drink far outstrips that of a human being; he will still be regaling the company with his stories long after every mortal present has passed out. He will then go on to empty all nearby casks and bottles, as well as the pantry (cluricauns have prodigious appetites), before taking his leave.

Because of their rather drunken and easy-going temperaments, cluricauns are extremely slow to anger; but when they are roused, their wrath can be quite fearsome. They can turn the milk completely sour overnight, prevent hens from laying, or inflict terrible wasting diseases upon a household. They can make cattle fall ill and sheep break out of their pens. They can cause minor disasters about a house — from the simple breaking of windows to the collapse of a chimney-stack. Although they will not willingly cause death, some of the sicknesses which they inflict can be very severe — poxes of various types, fevers, chills — and they can even cause dangerous accidents about the farmyard. It is, therefore, not wise to cross a cluricaun.

Alternatively, the cluricaun can bring good fortune to a house, if the mood takes him — this is not common, but it has been known to happen. Anticipating this, many householders will leave out a little piece of bread or a little saucer of milk or poteen for the fairy. This offering is meant to curry favour with the sprite and to keep him from raiding pantries or cellars. If the cluricaun is pleased with the gift, he may leave a coin (undoubtedly stolen from somewhere else) as payment, or he may simply lay a spell of good fortune on all the members of the household. In many cases, he will also act as the protector of the dwelling, seeing off evil spirits, ghosts and bad luck.

The cluricaun can often be much more capricious, temperamental and unpredictable than his leprechaun counterpart. In his drunken state, his mischief can sometimes get out of hand; for his own amusement, he will create mayhem throughout the house during the hours of darkness — overturning chairs, opening cupboards and wardrobes, pulling down plates and frightening the animals in their byres. It is doubtful whether he means any harm by this behaviour — it is usually put down to mere drunkenness — but he certainly can create a mess and much confusion. Not only this: the cluricaun, 'for sport', will also harness sheep, goats, cattle, sheepdogs and even domestic fowl, and ride them all through the countryside in a single night until the animals are dropping with fatigue and are fit for nothing. He will also break down fences and walls, and he often chases cattle through the countryside, making additional work for the farmer. Then, from the shadow of a sheltering hedge, with a jug of stolen poteen at his side, he will laugh at the mortals as they try to repair the damage he has caused. Again, the saying in the country is that 'there is no harm in him' and that he simply takes his mischief to excess, but there is no doubt that the cluricaun can cause great upset in any community.

Leprechauns have no great love or respect for their distant cousin, nor do they condone his 'pranks', for which they are frequently blamed. As has already been noted, leprechauns are not above such mischief themselves, but they usually only get up to it at certain times of the year (when they are at their most drunken); and they strongly object to being blamed for activities for which they are not actually responsible. Consequently, they tend to treat the cluricaun as a rogue and a scoundrel and refuse to acknowledge any form of kinship with him. They denounce his activities and treat him with a lofty disdain — particularly the more serious and academically inclined Connaught leprechauns, who tend to regard his inebriated escapades with the utmost horror. Some even deny that he exists at all!

Not that the cluricaun cares a fig about what they may think of him. He is out to enjoy himself if he can. Indeed, he may even go so far as to encourage the notion that has developed amongst some fairy-watchers — that cluricauns are nothing more than leprechauns out for 'drunken divilment'.

Sheela-na-Gigs

Although sheela-na-gigs are not really considered part of the fairy pantheon, there is a certain strand of Irish folklore which suggests that, in their initial form, they may be distantly related to the leprechaun. Academics, of course, will strenuously dispute this, claiming that they are representations of some aboriginal fertility goddess connected with reproduction and rebirth; but one is never sure. So it is probably wise to include some reference to them here.

Even though it has been asserted that there are now no female leprechauns, this may not always have been the case. Perhaps in some aboriginal time, when the fairy world was beginning to emerge out of its pre-historic past, there were female variants of a historically remote leprechaun ancestor. Some of these variants may even have survived down to the early medieval period, and may have had an influence upon early Christian religious art. Since then, however, they appear to have become completely extinct.

The name 'sheela-na-gig' comes from the Irish language, but its meaning and origin are uncertain. It may originally have been *síle na gcíoch*, taken to mean 'woman of the breasts', or *síle-ina-giob*, meaning 'an old woman on her hunkers', from the unusual squatting position of the figure. She is also known by a number of other names — Giddy Julia, St Shanahan, the Castle Hag, Sheila

O'Dwyer, or the Devil Stone or Devil Woman, to list but a few. She is usually depicted as a very small, very old woman, completely naked, crouching down with her thin arms wrapped round her knees. Her ribs sometimes show in an emaciated body, and in some carvings she seems to be completely bald.

Generally speaking, representations of sheela-na-gigs are to be found within churches and castles, and assume a close connection with these buildings. This is reminiscent of some leprechauns who, as we saw earlier, make their homes in ruined abbeys and abandoned houses. The name 'sheela-na-gig' was first used in the Proceedings of the Royal Irish Academy, 1840–1844, to describe the strange carved creature found on the gable wall of a church at Rochestown, County Tipperary. The name was also used in 1840 by John O'Donovan, official of the Ordnance Survey, to describe a similar carved figure on the wall of Kiltinane Church (also in Tipperary). Many other similar carvings are found in churches and great houses scattered throughout Ireland, showing the demographic spread of the tiny beings.

Neither Irish history nor folklore records what manner of creature is so depicted, or how she came to be incorporated in medieval Irish sculpture. Many people throughout Ireland believe that she may have been some sort of early fairy. There is an old legend concerning a stonemason named Rúairí O'Tunney, from the Kilkenny area, who was the finest mason of his day and who founded an entire Irish school of funerary monument design in the late fifteenth or early sixteenth century. He was allegedly taught all his skills by an extremely ancient female fairy-creature, whom he rewarded by placing her image all over Ireland, in his own work and in the work of his pupils. His style and imagery were copied by the later Ormond ornamental school, founded by one of the Butler Earls of Ormond in the 1600s. Might this 'elderly female fairy' who instructed the stonemason have been a sheela-na-gig, a sort of female leprechaun?

In Counties Cavan and Westmeath, these female creatures seem to have been quite ferocious; local representations of them show them to have teeth. A fanged being watches over a low gateway at the back of the castle in Moate, County Westmeath, set into an old wall which is thought to have been built around 1649. Similar carvings are to be seen at Lavey (County Cavan), Clonmel (County Tipperary) and Ballyporty (County Clare). Might these not have been guardians of the buildings, just as the cluricaun was regarded as a guardian in some more lowly Irish houses?

Certainly, such entities seem to provide a tangible connection between the medieval Christian world and the earlier pagan existence. These elderly leprechaun-like fairies may very well date from long before Christianity arrived in Ireland. One of the most ancient of these carved figures comes from Seir Kieran in County Offaly; it is carved in a monastic enclosure, which, in turn, was built upon the site of an extremely early Christian settlement (dated to as far back as 401 AD — thirty or so years before Patrick's arrival in Ireland). The carving was on the east gable of the Church of Ireland there, and its pagan presence so offended one of the clergy that he had it removed and sent to the National Museum in Dublin.

The Church may still be very uneasy about the close proximity of such fairy beings; it is said to have regarded them with some degree of abhorrence, but it nevertheless allowed them to be brought within its precincts and incorporated into its designs, in order that the holy influence of the site might either limit or extinguish their dark and evil powers.

Leprechauns, of course, with their usual disdain,

claim that sheela-na-gigs have never had anything to do with them, even in the remote and distant past. There never have been any females of their species whatsoever, they declare (thereby giving us our only clue to their origins). The carvings, leprechauns go on to say, are nothing more than creations of the medieval mind, and have more to do with humans than with fairies. Why else, they ask, would they be turning up in active Christian churches, where no leprechaun (let alone a fairy) would ever go?

And yet, even leprechauns appear to be a little afraid of the stone carvings; they are known to treat them with extreme reverence and respect when they encounter them in old ruins. Perhaps there is more of a connection between the two than we suspect!

Conclusion

Far from being simply an iconic representation of Ireland, the leprechaun is an extremely complex and contradictory being, to whom no amount of words will do justice. He is not a jolly and irrepressible cobbler — the stereotyped image by which he is usually portrayed. Leprechauns, as has hopefully been shown in this book, are surly and evasive creatures who will do mortals a bad turn just as quickly as a good one. They are frequently drunken and miserly, and even shun the company of other supernatural beings.

Leprechauns belong to a class of diminutive creatures that exist right across the world. They are related to the kobolds, the rock-trolls and other entities which live under the earth, which appear in the folklore of many nations. In England, for example, the leprechaun appears as Robin Goodfellow or Lob-lie-by-the-fire. In Wales, he appears as the bwca or brownie. In Germany, he is known as a hobgoblin — a little fellow who dwells by the hearth and who must be placated by members of the household. Amongst the Native Americans, as in Ireland, leprechaun-creatures are known as 'the little people of the mounds'. Perhaps, as we have suggested, there may be connections between them all.

So do leprechauns actually exist? Maybe they are the final vestige of some distant race memory of a smaller species which once coexisted with mankind. Maybe they are a vague recollection of ancient and powerful gods who were worshipped in some prehistoric time, and whose memory and stature have gradually diminished over the generations. Maybe they do exist and are out there lurking amongst the bushes and hedgerows of Ireland, waiting to play a trick or do some mischief.

Whether or not they are out there, leprechauns hold a powerful fascination for the Irish imagination (and that of other races as well). Despite their disagreeable ways and grudging attitude, there is something within their nature which sets them apart from other 'little folk', and which is attractive to the human psyche.

And, when you think about it, leprechauns have much to commend them.

Leprechauns are often unwashed and scruffy; but in an age where 'image is everything' and mortals are frequently judged upon the way they look rather than upon what is in their hearts, leprechauns show a refreshing absence of personal vanity.

They are careful with their money — which, when properly considered, is no great vice. Certainly they have a tremendous love for gold; but, unlike mortals, they do not despoil the environment to get at it. Indeed, they are the self-appointed guardians of the earth, taking revenge upon those who do it harm. And, in an age where natural things take a poor second place to capitalism and material expansion (which are often styled as 'development'), it is good to know that at least *someone* is keeping a eye on our world — even if it is not ourselves.

Leprechauns are the embodiment of the landscape, providing a sense of continuity from one age to the next. In an age where everything is transient, this is no bad thing. They provide a link between our own bustling reality and the more leisurely era of our forefathers — a sense of history and place. In a world where values are fast disappearing and where Time is master of us all, the leprechauns' approach to life is a thing to be treasured and nurtured.

The leprechaun, then, is more than a simple symbol of Ireland on a postcard, cup or tea-cloth. He is the representation of the deeper truths which often lie hidden — like the leprechaun himself — in the secret places of the Irish mind and heart.

BiBLioGRApHy

Briggs, Katherine, *A Dictionary of Fairies*, Penguin, 1976.

Campbell, A.A., *The Peat Fire's Flame*, Edinburgh, 1937.

Campbell, J.G., *Folktales from the West of Scotland*, Berlinn, 1998.

Carmichael, A., *Carmina Gadelica*, Floris, 1991.

Glassie, H., *Irish Folktales*, Penguin, 1993.

Curran, B., *Banshees, Beasts and Brides from the Sea*, Appletree Press, 1996.

Curran, B., *A Field Guide to Irish Fairies*, Appletree Press, 1998.

Curran, B., *Celtic Creatures — Mythologies and Folklore of the Western Celtic Empire*, Blandford, 2000.

Curtin, J., *Irish Fairy Tales*, Barnes & Noble, 1993.

Hyde, D., *Beside the Fire* (ed. Seamus Ó Duilearga), Irish Academic Press, 1978.

Kelly, E.P., *Sheela na Gigs — Origins and Functions*, Country House, 1996.

Kennedy, P., *Legends of Irish Witches and Fairies*, Mercier, 1991.

MacLellan, A., *Stories and Songs from South Uist*, Berlinn, 1998.

Macnamara, N., *Leprechaun Companion*, Pavilion, 1999.

Ó hÓgáin, D., *Myth, Legend and Romance — An Encyclopaedia of Irish Folk Tradition*, Prentice Hall, 1991.

Ó Súillebháin, S., 'The Folklore of Ireland', *The Folklore of the British Isles* (gen. ed. Venetia Newell), Batsford, 1974.

Thompson, F., *The Supernatural Highlands*, Luath, 1997.

Yeats, W.B., *Writings on Irish Folklore, Myth and Legend* (ed. R. Welch), Penguin, 1993.

BLOODY IRISH
Celtic Vampire Legends
BOB CURRAN

Contrary to popular belief, vampire stories originated in Ireland, including the most famous story, Bram Stoker's gothic masterpiece, *Dracula*. Centuries ago vampires cast their dark shadows across Celtic folklore. Bob Curran's four chilling stories reveal that vampires could still lurk beneath the surface of Irish life.

READ IF YOU DARE – BUT LEAVE ALL THE LIGHTS ON!

ISBN 1-903582-19-9

PROVERBS & SAYINGS OF IRELAND
Edited by Seán Gaffney and Seamus Cashman

An illustrated collection of over 1,000 proverbs, sayings and triads (arranged by subject) from all over Ireland.

Proverbs enable us to peer through the half-door, as it were, and glimpse the folk memories and philosophies of a people. Little escapes the barb but there is also humour and pride, faith and love – and the odd word of caution!

ISBN 0-86327-432-3

WOLFHOUND PRESS
An imprint of Merlin Publishing
16 Upper Pembroke Street, Dublin 2, Ireland
Tel: +353 1 676 4373 Fax: +353 1 676 4368
publishing@merlin.ie
www.merlin-publishing.com